TRUTH SPEAKS TO POWER

The Countercultural Nature of Scripture

WALTER BRUEGGEMANN

WJK WESTMINSTER
JOHN KNOX PRESS
LOUISVILLE · KENTUCKY

© 2013 Walter Brueggemann

First edition
Published by Westminster John Knox Press
Louisville, Kentucky

13 14 15 16 17 18 19 20 21 22—10 9 8 7 6 5 4 3 2 1

Unless otherwise indicated, Scripture quotations are from the New Revised Standard Version of the Bible, copyright © 1989 by the Division of Christian Education of the National Council of the Churches of Christ in the U.S.A., and used by permission. Italic emphasis has been added by the author.

Book design by Erika Lundbom
Cover design by designpointinc.com

Library of Congress Cataloging-in-Publication Data

Brueggemann, Walter.
    Truth speaks to power / Walter Brueggemann. — 1st ed.
      p. cm.
    ISBN 978-0-664-23914-5 (alk. paper)
    1. Bible. O.T.—Theology.   2. Bible—Criticism, interpretation, etc.
3. Power (Christian theology)—Biblical teaching.   4. Truth—Biblical
teaching.   I. Title.
    BS1192.5.B83 2013
    230'.0411—dc23

                                 2012032985

CONTENTS

Foreword by Thomas Breidenthal   *v*

Introduction   1

1. Truth Speaks to Power: Moses   11

2. Visible Power, Truth Cunningly
   Subversive: Solomon   43

3. Truth Has Its Day: Elisha   81

4. Truth Transforms Power: Josiah   113

5. Power and Truth among Us   149

FOREWORD

ABOUT FOUR YEARS AGO I OPENED A NOTE FROM WALTER Brueggemann letting me know that he was moving to the Cincinnati area, would be attending an Episcopal congregation, and stood ready to be helpful to the Diocese of Southern Ohio. I could hardly believe it. I had been following Dr. Brueggemann's biblical studies since the early nineties, when, as an assistant professor at General Theological Seminary, I was electrified by his exposition of the psalms of lament. I trust he doesn't regret his offer to be a resource for the diocese, for we certainly have taken him up on it. Brueggemann has led clergy days; keynoted regional conferences; participated in numerous study series at his parish, at our Cathedral, and elsewhere; and offered invaluable advice to me in my own work. Throughout this time it has been my honor to get to know him and his wife, Tia, personally.

As Brueggemann mentions, this book arises out of a group of lectures delivered at a summer conference jointly sponsored by the two Episcopal dioceses in Ohio. In my view, *Truth Speaks to Power* represents his boldest exploration to date of the radical and subversive political implications of the Bible. Although Brueggemann insists that no direct line can be drawn from the Bible to any particular political agenda, he clearly discerns a persistent point of view in the "song, oracle, and narrative" of Scripture, which—although he does not say this outright—might be taken to constitute its unity as a canon. This viewpoint comes down to a suspicion of truth claims that support vested power interests and an irrepressible conviction that God's truth stands on the side of the weak, the poor, and the excluded. Although the Bible may not endorse any particular political agenda, it places in question any agenda that protects the privilege of some at the expense of others. Brueggemann pulls no punches in naming the habitual collusion of government; the corporate world; the media; the academy; and, yes, the church to control the definition of truth and shut out (or co-opt) any narrative voices that object. His thesis—or warning—is that when we pay close attention to what is going on in the biblical text, even when it may seem to be in support of the status quo of its time, we will perceive an authorial voice, sometimes passionate, sometimes deadpan, that refuses worldly power's party line then *and* now.

This is not to say that Brueggemann invites us to approach the Bible naively, as if its meaning were always obvious and its guidance straightforward. Brueggemann's genius is to introduce us into a biblical terrain that is complex and gnarly, constituted by layer on layer of contested story. But for him the bedrock of that ground is the twofold conviction that God is not reducible to human power agendas and that the neighbor is made in the image of God. When we read and hear Scripture with attention, even the difficulties—the contradictions, about-faces, violence, and maddening silences—will lead us eventually to that truth. This is not to say that we don't bring our own interpretative lens to what we read and hear. But it *is* to say that when we are engaged with Scripture we are on holy ground. This holy ground is both as strange and as familiar as the contradictions, failures, and graces of our own lives, which can hurl us unexpectedly into the truth of neighbor-as-God. It is also as strange and familiar as what Brueggemann calls the "lyrical" Christian assertion that in Jesus the "high God" and the "lowly neighbor" are one.

Beyond the assertion of this ground, Brueggemann resists systematization. Anyone who has experienced him in person as a teacher knows that he simply wants to awaken us to the riches, enigmas, and affronts that any text of Scripture will present us with. His teacherly voice—at times guilefully folksy, at times powerfully personal, at all times learned—can be heard throughout this book. Enter and be taught.

Bishop Thomas E. Breidenthal
Episcopal Church, Diocese of Southern Ohio

INTRODUCTION

THE MATERIAL THAT FOLLOWS GREW OUT OF AN INVITATION I happily received from the Episcopal Diocese of Southern Ohio to teach in a summer lay event to be held at Kenyon College. The invitation suggested presentations on faith and the public sector. I do not recall the exact wording of the invitation, but it suggested an interface between biblical faith and public policy, or, perhaps more likely, the way in which biblical faith is concerned with questions of social justice and the consequent mandate to social action.

I do not believe that the Bible points directly to any political policy or action . . . nor did my hosts have that in mind. I believe that, at the most, the Bible (a) can frame questions in the public sector according to the will and purpose of God as that will and purpose have been discerned in the church in a long, interpretive tradition and (b) can provide specific materials that may evoke and tilt our imagination in one direction or another. Thus I do not believe that one can make direct moves toward or connections with contemporary issues, even though we—liberals and conservatives—keep trying to do just that.

It is for that reason that I have reframed the invitation around the interface of power and truth with the thought that public power is everywhere wielded and administered by those with concentrations of wealth, who thereby control the supply of money, who control the legislation that governs credit and debt, and who fund (or refuse to fund) military adventurism and technological advances that are often in the service of the military. Thus *power* refers to a network of influence and leverage that may be channeled through the state apparatus or, as is the case in our society, through the private sector with its huge corporate combines. Either way, such concentrations of power rely as Karl Marx understood, on the "symbolizers" (the church, the academy, and the media) to legitimate the use of power. All of which is summarized in the popular version of the Golden Rule: The ones with the gold make the rules.

The counterpoint for this presentation is truth that is not so easy to come by. In my earlier book on David, I identified several David narratives: the truth of the tribe, the truth of the man, the truth of the state, and the truth of the church (assembly).[1] While that presentation may have been a bit overly schematic, the inventory that I proposed suggested that the several narratives testimonies to David offer distinct versions of the truth about David, each of which is permeated with vested interest. The variety of testimonies makes clear that the truth about David is deeply and endlessly contested. It is equally clear that society, then and now, characteristically traffics in established truth about which there is general agreement among the parties that matter: the state, the church, the corporate structure, the academy, and so on. These several institutions are skillful in articulating and maintaining truth that can readily be seen as allied with status quo power.

But of course there are other versions of truth, the kind that arise from below, that are carried by nonexperts, people without credentials. The truth from below lives very close to actual concrete existence, just as official truth may often be a great distance removed from actual lived experience. In his study of the weak, James C. Scott, with reference to "hidden scripts," has proposed that peasant truth is closely linked to lived reality and mostly kept hidden from the practitioners of official truth.[2]

In the Bible one can see this same taxonomy of truth. In the Old Testament, official truth is carried by the urban elites of dynasty and temple and eventually by the scribal class.[3] And in the New Testament, the same truth is variously carried and sustained by the scribal community that is allied with other establishment parties. In both testaments, however, there is another truth. In the Old Testament, that other truth is carried by song, oracle, and narrative that continually subvert official truth. In the communities that produced the text, that subversion must have been both valued and enjoyed, and that subversive potential continues to be operative in the rereading of the texts. In the New Testament, that counter-truth is carried by Jesus and his followers, a community that regularly and with great risk subverts and bewilders the establishment and so turns the "world upside down" (Acts 17:6). As a consequence, truth, unlike establishment power that is visible, is characteristically elusive and contested because the claims made for truth are variously endorsements of or subversions of established power. The occupants of power are, of necessity, always seeking out versions of truth that are compatible with present power arrangements. Conversely, outsiders to present power arrangements are always proposing a counter-truth that will permit and legitimate counter-arrangements of power.

The issue of truth and power, of course, takes a different form in the modern history of the West. The official truth, in the modern West, is of a Cartesian kind in which rational knowledge amounts to power over the economy, over scientific/technological pursuits, and over knowledge so that the military-industrial-educational-media complex can claim a monopoly of all-important truth. That monopoly serves to maintain the status quo in a totalizing system that will legitimate nothing outside its purview.

As might be expected, such a totalizing combination of truth and power is bound to evoke counterforces who refuse to accept the closed account of thin modern rationality. These "masters of suspicion," as Paul Ricouer labeled them, pay attention to the incontrovertible bodily reality that continues to speak against the flat claims of thin reason. Ricoeur focuses on Freud, but he includes in his roster of the masters Karl Marx and Friedrich Nietzsche. He allows that what they have in common is more important than the differences that we characteristically accent. First he notes their "common opposition" in their critique of domain culture: All three masters "contest the primacy of the object in our representation of the sacred, as well as the fulfilling of the intention of the sacred by a type of analogy of being that would engraft us onto being through the power of an assimilating intention. It is also easy to recognize that this contesting is an exercise of suspicion in three different ways; 'truth as lying' would be the negative heading under which one might place these three exercises of suspicion."[4]

Ricoeur obverses that we have not fully appreciated "the positive meaning" that the three have in common: a perspective of false consciousness.

> All three clear the horizon for a more authentic word, for a new reading of Truth, not only by means of a "destructive" critique, but by the invention of an art of *interpreting*. . . . What must be faced, therefore, is not only a threefold suspicion, but a threefold guile. If consciousness is not what it thinks it is, a new relation must be instituted between the patent and the latent; this new relation would correspond to the one that consciousness had instituted between appearance and the reality of things.[5]

Ricoeur concludes:

> At issue in this controversy is the fate or what I shall call, for the sake of brevity, the mytho-poetic core of imagination. . . . And does not this grace of imagination have something to do with the Word as Revelation?[6]

Thus Karl Marx, by his distinction of "base" and "superstructure," exposed the high claims of "established truth" as distanced from material, bodily reality. That distance (alienation) he slotted as "false consciousness"—the truth of established society that was cut off from the pain and suffering of much elemental economic reality. Nietzsche famously characterized "truth" as an "army of metaphors." By that he meant that truth is not a given, but it is an elusive, contested act of interpretation that emerges and makes claims through many twists and turns. And Freud, with his theory of repression, identified the subterranean reality of the unconscious that we keep in place by denial in the service of the status quo.[7] The more recent heir of these masters is Michel Foucault, who has seen, in a most compelling way, the enmeshment of truth and power with each other.[8]

The sum of these masters of suspicion is to protest against reasonable truth that is featured by established power and to insist that there is another more elemental, more bodily truth that hovers beneath what is acceptable and that continues to haunt social reality, no matter how much we pretend and insist otherwise. To be sure, the exposé of modernist reason in these proponents of truthfulness is cast in a rhetoric that is remote from and strange to biblical faith.

For good reason, however, the case is often and readily made that the suspicion practiced by these masters is fully congruent with the subversive voice of Scripture, most notably in the prophets, but everywhere voiced in song, narrative, and oracle. Thus the Bible itself is a sustained contestation over truth in which conventional modes of power do not always prevail. My purpose in these chapters is to invite the reader to participate in that contestation that is under way in the text itself. Thus being the interpreter, as a "contestant," is an inescapable role because we have before us competing claims to truth—some attached to power, some arraigned against power—about which decisions must be made as we read and interpret.

I should note two other factors that are important for what follows. First, biblical testimony, as pertains to social power, is deeply and cunningly ironic. If we read the Bible innocently—either according to conventional church categories or conventional historical criticism, we are likely to miss what is going on in the text as far as the Bible asserts truth that challenges power. When we notice the irony, we notice that the text speaks, perforce, in a double dialect. On the one hand, its language may be taken at face value by the innocent reader; on the other hand, what lies beneath the text contradicts the apparent meaning of a face-value reading. But then, subversives in the face of totalism have always had to speak twice in the same utterance, once for the official record and once for the truth of bodily reality. Thus when we read beneath we can see how the assumed authority of power is undermined in cunning and compelling ways. Carolyn Sharp shrewdly characterizes irony in this way:

> Irony is a performance of misdirection that generates aporetic interactions between an unreliable "said" and a truer "unsaid" so as to persuade us of something that is subtler, more complex, and more profound than the apparent meaning. Irony disrupts cultural assumptions about the narrative coherence that seems to ground tropological and epistemological transitions, inviting us into an experience of alterity that moves us toward new insight by problematizing false understandings.[9]

Sharp calls attention to an experience of alterity whereby the contestant becomes aware of alternative ways of power that are grounded in alternative voicings of truth. The modern master of irony, Wayne Booth, speaks of the "secret communion" of author and reader who share an "understanding" that is not on the surface of the world.[10] Booth has elsewhere suggested that irony is the modern mode whereby idolatry is exposed and idols are dethroned; in our context, the idols of totalizing claims of power. Sharp's more recent study of the biblical texts (where Booth does not go very much) has shown the pervasive force of irony in the biblical text that continues its subversive insistence. It may well be that irony is the vehicle for traducing the unsettled space between truth and power, for truth readily subverts power in the exposé of irony.[11]

Second, the case studies I offer in what follows might suggest to an alert reader something of a taxonomy like that of H. Richard Niebuhr in his classic study, *Christ and Culture*. While such modeling is possible on the basis of what I have written, I want to disclaim any intention of modeling a taxonomy. Rather the texts I have chosen for discussion are one-off enactments from which generalizations should not be drawn. Of course we do draw such generalizations from specific instances and find parallels of which there are many. That, however, is not my intent. I prefer, rather, to invite the reader into the thick complexity of the textual particularity. What is made of such particularity after that work is done is the responsibility of the reader, a responsibility that goes beyond my own insistence. I hope, mainly, to exhibit the thick complexity of the interface of truth and power in which we ourselves are always engaged, and to insist that we are, as readers and interpreters, always contestants, whether we recognize ourselves as such or not.

NOTES

1. Walter Brueggemann, *David's Truth in Israel's Imagination and Memory* (Philadelphia: Fortress Press, 1985).

2. James C. Scott, *Weapons of the Weak: Everyday Forms of Peasant Resistance* (New Haven, CT: Yale University Press, 1985); and Scott, *Domination and the Arts of Resistance: Hidden Transcripts* (New Haven: Yale University Press, 1990).

3. See Philip R. Davies, *Scribes and Schools: The Canonization of the Hebrews Scriptures* (Louisville, KY: Westminster John Knox Press, 1998).

4. Paul Ricoeur, *Freud and Philosophy: An Essay on Interpretation* (New Haven, CT: Yale University Press, 1970), 32.

5. Ibid., 32–33.
6. Ibid., 35–36.
7. The defining power of the unconscious would seem to be a rediscovery of David Brooks, *The Social Animal: The Hidden Sources of Love, Character, and Achievement* (New York: Random House, 2011).
8. On Michael Foucault, see Barry Cooper, *Michel Foucault: An Introduction to the Study of His Thought* (New York: Mellan, 1982). There you will also find an extended list of Foucault's writings.
9. Carolyn J. Sharp, *Irony and Meaning in the Hebrew Bible* (Bloomington: Indiana University Press, 2009), 24.
10. Wayne C. Booth, *The Rhetoric of Fiction,* 2nd ed. (Chicago: Chicago University Press, 1983), 300.
11. On irony amid the totalizing claims of U.S. history, see Reinhold Niebuhr, *The Irony of American History* (New York: Charles Scribner's, 1952).

Chapter 1

TRUTH SPEAKS TO POWER

Moses

WHEN WE COME TO THE INTERFACE OF *PUBLIC POWER* AND *PUBLIC truth*, the Old Testament is an indispensable reference point. Because the exodus story is the pivot for faith claims in the Old Testament, we are plunged immediately into public dimensions of power and truth.[1] And after the exodus narrative, the prophetic tradition keeps us intensely focused on public issues. The questions of justice and order and freedom and peace never go away in ancient Israel. Conversely it is clear that without reference to the Old Testament, the New Testament can be carried way into privatism and matters of spirituality without reference to the public good.[2] Indeed, the religious settlement of the Enlightenment has confined Christian faith to the private sphere in a wholesale retreat from public issues.

While matters are acutely complex, it is clear that we now face a profound crisis concerning the public good and the administration of public power and public resources.[3] On the one hand, Christian faith has largely retreated to private, domestic, residential matters. On the other hand, market ideology goes unchecked in the public square, devouring the poor, eradicating the force of organized labor, and abusing the environment in violent ways.

Grounded in the Old Testament narrative and the prophetic tradition, and in response to that crisis of acquisitive greed, the church is, in my judgment, called to its public vocation to practice neighborliness in a way that includes both support of policies of distributive justice and practices of face-to-face restorative generosity.[4] I dare to imagine that the connection between this ancient textual tradition of *public imagination* and our current *social crisis* is pivotal for the faithfulness of the church. It is this textual tradition, like none other, that can lead the church to imagine (and practice) the world as a neighborhood network of mutual respect and concern, and not simply as a market of detached competitors.[5]

By way of entry into our theme of power and truth, and part of our specific topic in this chapter, "Truth Speaks to Power," I appeal to the remarkable narrative of Jesus on trial before Pilate in the Fourth Gospel (John 18:28–19:16), a narrative that, as we will see, echoes the exodus story. The editors of the NRSV have provided a superscription for this narrative, "Jesus before Pilate." In a typical flat, uninspired reading of Scripture, they propose a very conventional label for the narrative. It would require a much more daring interpretive move to label it, as Paul Lehmann has done, "Pilate before Jesus."[6] The narrative is very cagey about whom it is who is on trial, but clearly Pilate is placed at risk by the narrative and by the conduct of Jesus. Pilate is the agent and representative of the Roman Empire who presides over organized power in that colonial society. The narrative gives ample space to the direct, confrontive exchange between this *cipher of imperial power* and this *carrier of foundational truth* who will address that power. Indeed, the "court record" as given here is a charged reflection on the nature of public power. There is the initial exploratory exchange between the Roman governor and the company of colluding Jews who are for a time identified only as an unidentified "they" (18:28–32). But then the governor comes face to face with the accused. The governor asks him,

"Are you the King of the Jews?" (v. 33)

Jesus parries:

"Is that your own question, or did they tell you to ask it?" (v. 34, au. trans.).

The governor defends himself by distinguishing himself from the Jews as an officer of the empire, as though to remind Jesus whom he addresses just in case it had slipped his mind that this is the greatest empire in the history of the world, the last standing superpower. He reminds Jesus that he is in court because he is charged by "your own nation and the chief priests" (v. 35), that is, by the colluders among the colonized people. And then the governor cuts to the chase: "'What have you done?'" (v.35).

Jesus responds in an elusive way:

"My kingdom is not from this world. If my kingdom were from this world, my followers would be fighting to keep me from being handed over to the Jews. But as it is, my kingdom is not from here." (v. 26)

Jesus has spoken twice of "my kingdom." As a result, we are not surprised that the governor picks up on the inflammatory phrase, "my kingdom," and draws the conclusion: "So you are a king?" (v. 37).

Jesus parries again, as though to say, "You might say that."

> "You say that I am a king. For this I was born, and for this I came into the world, to testify to the truth. Everyone who belongs to the truth listens to my voice." (v. 37)

And then Pilate, in frustration or in defiance, in his demanding authority or in yielding disease asks: "'What is truth?'" (v. 38).

We do not know the tone of his question. But clearly the entire narrative has been moving toward this wonderment. And then, as though to close the hearing, Pilate reports back to the Jewish authorities: "'I find no case against the man'" (v. 38).

Jesus is exonerated by the empire, even against the will of the colluding Jewish leadership. But now the governor has voiced the lingering, unanswered question, "What is truth?" Here is the empire in bewilderment, the empire that had postured in all its certitude and authority beyond challenge, now conceding that what it has most championed it could not sustain.

Jesus had already declared to his disciples, "'I am the way, the truth, and the life'" (14:6). He had already announced that he was the truth. But of course the governor was not privy to that declaration given only to Jesus' inner circle. Nor would Pilate have understood it if he had heard it, because the claim would have eluded his imperial categories.

In this narrative we have, as Paul Lehmann has seen, the pivotal contest of biblical faith between power and truth:

> The rupture of the self-justification of power by the calling into question of all power, forces the use and validation of power back to the question of the ultimate point and purpose of power. This is the question of truth. Thus the nocturnal conversation between Jesus and Pilate turns into a confrontation. In this confrontation, the ambiguity of power and the ambiguity of Presence are juxtaposed. The ambiguity of power is that power cannot of itself fulfill or justify itself. The ambiguity of Presence is that it is at once concretely *there* in the world of time and space and things and an invasion of that world from another world, the world of origin and destiny, of an originating purpose and a purposed fulfillment. . . . The point and purpose of the presence of Jesus *in the world*, and now before Pilate, are to bear witness to the truth that is, "to make effective room for the reality of God over against the world in the great trial between God and the world."[7]

Lehmann makes a great deal out of the silence of Jesus before the demands of Pilate. Jesus has no need to answer to Pilate. By his silence Jesus converts Pilate's questions into an exposé of Pilate's fraudulent power. Thus truth, as it is embodied in Jesus, problematizes the power of Pilate and of Rome. And so it always is with truth when it is an enactment of God's presence in the world. Power that has been founded on something other than that truth is exposed as fraudulent, delegitimized power.

The narrative engagement of Jesus with Pilate becomes a screen through which we may rediscern the interface of power and truth in our own social setting. Power among us is now exhibited as the unfettered, aggressive acquisitiveness of a can-do society. It is a force that regards itself as autonomous and beyond restraint or limit. It does indeed sweep all before it. And in its face, the church holds this narrative, this presence, and this claim that always appear vulnerable and without force. It is an unequal contest that is narrated in the Fourth Gospel. And it is always and again the same unequal context that concerns those who consider the force of gospel truth in the public domain.

ESSENTIAL CHARACTERS IN THE EXODUS STORY

But of course the narrative of the Fourth Gospel is not original in the imagination of God's people. Rather, it is an echo and reiteration of Israel's paradigmatic narrative power and truth, the exodus narrative. It is to this narrative that Jews—and consequently Christians—always return, because it provides for us the *essential characters* and the *recurring plot* that is always being performed and reperformed in the world. The narrative depends on the participation and performance of *four characters* who always make appearance in the drama of power and truth.

Pharaoh

There is *Pharaoh*, always Pharaoh, at the center of the world of power. Pharaoh is (or is taken to be by historical criticism) an actual historical character, variously identified as Sethos, Ramses II, or Merneptah, depending on when one dates the exodus event.[8] Or perhaps the capacity to identify the Pharaoh of the narrative belongs only to an earlier fideistic mode of critical scholarship, since the historicity of the narrative is now in much greater doubt. It is at least observable that the narrative never gives a name to him. He

is never named, perhaps because he is not the lead character in the narrative, even if he is indispensable for the plot.
More likely, in my judgment, he is never named because he
could have been any one of a number of candidates, or all
of them. Because if you have seen one pharaoh, you have
seen them all. They all act the same way in their greedy,
uncaring, violent self-sufficiency.

Whatever we are to say of his identity as a historical
character, Pharaoh is clearly a metaphor. He embodies and
represents raw, absolute, worldly power. He is, like Pilate
after him, a stand-in for the whole of the empire. As the
agent of the "empire of force," he reappears in many different personae.[9]

He has a food monopoly, and "food is a weapon";[10] here it
is a weapon used by Pharaoh against Pharaoh's own people:

> So Joseph bought all the land of Egypt for Pharaoh. All
> the Egyptians sold their fields, because the famine was
> severe upon them; and the land became Pharaoh's. As for
> the people, he made slaves of them from one end of Egypt
> to the other. Only the land of the priests he did not buy;
> for the priests had a fixed allowance from Pharaoh, and
> lived on the allowance that Pharaoh gave them; therefore
> they did not sell their land. Then Joseph said to the people,
> "Now that I have this day bought you and your land for
> Pharaoh, here is the seed for you; sow the land. And at
> the harvests you shall give one-fifth to Pharaoh, and four-
> fifths shall be your own, as seed for the field and as food for
> yourselves and your households, and as food for your little
> ones." (Gen. 47:20–24)

From the outset, Pharaoh, blessed by God's Nile,
was the leader of the breadbasket of the world (see Gen.
12:10). By his own actions and those of his food czar,
Joseph, Pharaoh advanced the claims of the state against

his own subjects, achieving a monopoly on land and on the food supply. That land and food supply became a tax base whereby wealth was systematically transferred from the peasant-slaves to the central monopoly.

Because Pharaoh has so much food, he needs granaries in which to store his surplus. The construction of such storehouses for surplus was the work of those who were forced by famine into slave labor:

> Therefore they set taskmasters over them to oppress them with forced labor. They built supply cities, Pithom and Rameses, for Pharaoh. (Exod. 1:11)

The narrative does not miss the irony that those forced by *famine* into slavery are engaged in storing then *surplus* of the empire. It is astonishing that critical scholarship has asked forever about the identification of these store-house cities, but without ever asking about the skewed exploitative social relationships between owner and laborers that the project exhibits. The store-house cities are an ancient parallel to the great banks and insurance houses where surplus wealth is kept among us. That surplus wealth, produced by the cheap labor of peasants, must now be protected from the peasants by law and by military force.

Pharaoh's great accumulation of wealth—in land and in food—is the outcome of cheap labor. The cunning food administration plans of Joseph have created for Pharaoh a peasant underclass of very cheap labor. The narrative knows the way in which hungry peasants, in need of food from the monopoly, will pay their money, then forfeit their cattle, and then finally give up their land, because Pharaoh leverages food in order to enhance his power. In the end, the peasants are so "happy" that they asked to be "owned":

Buy us and our land in exchange for food. We with our land will become slaves to Pharaoh; just give us seed, so that we may live and not die, and that the land may not become desolate. (Gen. 47:19)

By the end of the narrative they are grateful to be cast as cheap labor for Pharaoh: "'You have saved our lives; may it please my lord, we will be slaves to Pharaoh'" (v. 25).

Pharaoh's exploitation of cheap labor is without restraint. He is propelled by insatiable greed. He has more food to store; and so he needs more granaries; and to have more granaries, he must have more bricks out of which they are to be constructed. Thus, Exodus 5 presents the production schedule for brick-making that is ruthless and without any slippage or accommodation:

"Why are you taking the people away from their work? Get to your labors." (v. 4)

"Now they are more numerous than the people of the land and yet you want them to stop working!" (v. 5)

"You shall no longer give the people straw to make bricks as before; let them go and gather straw for themselves. But you shall require of them the same quantity of bricks as they have made previously; do not diminish it, for they are lazy; that is why they cry, 'Let us go and offer sacrifice to our God.' Let heavier work be laid on them; then they will labor at it and pay no attention to deceptive words." (vv. 7–9)

"Thus says Pharaoh: 'I will not give you straw. Go and gather straw yourselves, wherever you can find it; but our work will not be lessened in the least.'" (vv. 10–11)

"Complete your work, the same daily assignment as when you were given straw." (v. 13)

"Why did you not finish the required quantity of bricks yesterday and today, as you did before?" (v. 14)

"Why do you treat your servants like this? No straw is given to your servants, yet they say to us, 'Make bricks!' Look how your servants are beaten! You are unjust to your own people. . . . You are lazy, lazy; that is why you say, 'Let us go and sacrifice to the LORD.' Go now, and work; for no straw shall be given you but you shall still deliver the same number of bricks." (vv. 15–18)

"You shall not lessen your daily number of bricks." (v. 19)

The slaves had no rights, no protectors or guarantors; they are completely vulnerable to the unchecked power of Pharaoh.

For all of that, Pharaoh is consumed with anxiety. Likely it is the same anxiety that produced the nightmare of scarcity back in Genesis 41:

Then seven other cows, ugly and thin, came up out of the Nile after them, and stood by the other cows on the bank of the Nile . . . The ugly and thin cows ate up the seven sleek and fat cows. . . . Then seven ears, thin and blighted by the east wind, sprouted after them. The thin ears swallowed up the seven plump and full ears. (Gen. 41:3-7)

Now, in his fear, Pharaoh resolves to destroy the children of the slaves, that is, the next generation of his cheap labor. On the one hand, he decided to drive them crazy with exploitative work expectations:

The Egyptians became ruthless in imposing tasks on the Israelites, and made their lives bitter with hard service in mortar and brick and in every kind of field labor. They were ruthless in all the tasks that they imposed on them. (Exod. 1:13–14)

On the other hand, Pharaoh resolved to kill all the baby boys among the slave community:

"When you act as midwives to the Hebrew women and see them on the birthstool, if it is a boy, kill him; but if it is a girl, she shall live." (Exod. 1:16)

The narrative does not comment on the irony here, as in Genesis 41, that the one *with the most* is the one who is *most anxious* in irrational ways. His anxiety in Genesis 41 is unrelated to the reality of his food supply. And his anxiety here leads to self-destructive policies that contradict his own stated needs. Without calling attention to it, the narrative shows the way in which unrestrained power becomes destructive, both for those subject to that power and, eventually, for those who exercise such power as well.

The Hebrew Peasants

The second character in the narrative, presented as an undifferentiated group, without name or face, are *the Hebrew peasants* who have been reduced to slavery. They are completely in the service of the raw, ambitious power of Pharaoh, acted on rather than being actors. They have become slaves of that monopolizing power in a trade-off for food that they had to have in order to live. They have, of necessity, forfeited their bodies to the empire; characteristically the empire will use their bodies without regret or acknowledgement. Pharaoh will do so because, from his perspective, it is all about the economy, about cheap labor and production and scarcity and surplus, surely enough to assuage his anxiety! The slaves are the ones who will make the continuing food monopoly of the Pharaoh possible; they do not benefit at all from their hard labor because their assigned purpose is to produce security and happiness for Pharaoh.

As the narrative advances, however, a quite remarkable turn takes place. The silent slaves, pawns of Pharaoh, find their voice. They did not find their voice until Pharaoh died, the one who had been ruthless toward them. But of course, after Pharaoh died, there will be another pharaoh, because there is always another pharaoh. In the face of this new pharaoh (who is, of course, unnamed), they find voice. They become agents in their own history, paying attention to their bodily pain and finding voice to match their pain: "After a long time the king of Egypt died. The Israelites groaned under their slavery and cried out" (Exod. 2:23).

It is this remarkable act on the part of the slaves that set the narrative of history in motion. Most remarkably, in the early chapters of Exodus, YHWH makes no appearance in the text until it is time to respond to the cry of the slaves:

> Out of their slavery their cry for help rose up to God. God heard their groaning, and God remembered his covenant with Abraham, Isaac, and Jacob. God looked upon the Israelites, and God took notice of them. (Exod. 2:23–25)

It is the voice of the slaves, newly sounded, that draws YHWH actively into the narrative.

YHWH

It is this *YHWH*, now activated by the cries of cheap labor, who becomes a key player in the story. This character is creator of heaven and earth. He is the one, we confess, who is "The Father, the Son, and the Spirit," fully present, fully engaged, fully participant in this circumstance of abuse and need. YHWH waits two long chapters before entering the narrative. YHWH comes late to the crisis of the empire. If we were not so familiar with it, we might ask, as Bible readers, "What took so long? Where have you been?" Perhaps the answer is that YHWH waited to be summoned by human cries. YHWH waited until there was acknowledgment and articulation of bodily human pain. Perhaps YHWH waited until there was human protest against raw power before there was an opening and a role for YHWH to play. In any case, when YHWH at long last enters the narrative, YHWH will become the big player.

Over time, as we will see, YHWH grows more and more decisive in the narrative, even as Pharaoh recedes to irrelevance.[11] This YHWH who comes anew to the slaves is not fully a *novum* by the time Israel has completed its tradition.[12] When God enters the exodus narrative, YHWH comes directly out of the book of Genesis. Back there in the narratives of Genesis YHWH had been making promises to the ancestors. It is for that reason that YHWH responded to the cries of the cheap day-laborers by remembering ancient promises. It was also the case, however, that YHWH had been dormant (or absent or disengaged) from Israel for a long while—all through the Joseph narrative. That may well be because Joseph—now the fourth generation after Abraham, Isaac, and Jacob—had turned his life toward the pharaoh and away from YHWH. For good reason, Leon Kass judges that Joseph was fully "Egyptianized."[13] The God of promises may have been unwelcome in such an imperial environment. Even given such a sabbatical from promise-keeping, YHWH now enters this exodus narrative with vigor and authority.

Moses

The fourth character is *Moses*, so named, we are told, because he was "drawn" out of the water.

He has an unreported childhood after a fear-laden birth story. That secret childhood has given large room for speculation about an Egyptian, royal upbringing; Egyptian monotheism; and all manner of daring thought. Suffice it to say that the narrative has no interest in such speculation. And of course the narrative knows that YHWH, the God of the narrative, cannot be extrapolated from any antecedent Egyptian monotheism. YHWH is a *novum* in the narrative, underived and unexplained. The narrative turns our attention away from speculation about the childhood of Moses to the emergence of the adult Moses.

Whatever may have been his Egyptian rootage (about which we know nothing), that rootage is not defining for the adult character of Moses in this narrative. His first adult appearance in the narrative occurs when he goes out to "his people" and observes "their forced labor" (2:11). The pronouns are important. From the outset Moses is identified with the slave-labor force; his identity and his commitment are not in doubt. He lives in the context of forced labor. He sees a "brother" being abused by an Egyptian, an agent of Pharaoh's exploitative policies. No doubt the beating of the slave by the Egyptian was because the slave was not working hard enough or was recalcitrant against imperial authority. In any case, Moses—either as a freedom fighter for his people or as a terrorist against established authority, or both—kills the Egyptian agent of Pharaoh. Moses is ready to intervene against the empire on behalf of the exploited.

Having struck a blow against the empire, Moses is a fugitive. Pharaoh, it is reported, "sought to kill" him (2:15). Moses from now on is completely resistant to the power of Pharaoh.

These four characters are bound together in this tension-filled drama of power and truth. Israel insists, in its telling, that all four characters matter decisively. If Israel does not tell the story, we will lose some of the characters. If the story is told from the perspective of economic reality, it may be reduced to Pharaoh and the slaves—that is, to capital and labor. Or alternatively, it could be told as a tale of order and terror. Or if the conventional church tells the story, it may become a tale of God and Israel and God's great love for Israel; but Pharaoh disappears in that telling, and even Israel is taken more as the beloved of God than as cheap labor in the empire. Or if one wants to tell a "great-man theory" of history, we have Moses, the great emancipator, but without the YHWH force behind him.[14]

Israel, in its telling, presents a map of power and truth that focuses on the two characters that drop out of conventional economic analysis, even as the conventional church downplays the economic dimension:

- *YHWH* presides and makes *Pharaoh* penultimate; Pharaoh is essential to the narrative, but only so that he can be dismissed and ridiculed.
- *Moses* is offered as a summoned human agent in the struggle for truth with power in a way that makes the cosmic struggle an altogether human context of *slave labor.*

This map of power with its four characters is replicated in the narrative of the Fourth Gospel to which I have alluded.

- There is *Pilate,* surrogate of Caesar and surely as much an agent of the empire as was Pharaoh. Like Pharaoh, Pilate is inured with power but could not fathom the question of truth. Pilate is abetted by the high priests, who are Jewish but who fully collude with the power of the empire.

- There is *the rabid mob* that liked to say things twice for emphasis. In response to Pilate's query about releasing Jesus, they say, "Not this man, but Barabbas" (John 18:40). And in 19:15, when Pilate wants to release Jesus, they say, "Away with him! Away with him!"; in 19:6, they say, "Crucify him! Crucify him!" This mob as a character is not an equivalent to the slaves who are the fourth character in the exodus narrative. They are important, however, because they are the unwitting agents of the empire, the base that exercises vocal leverage that turns out to be a support for the status quo and the enhancement of the powers that be.
- There is, third, this *Jesus,* who must appear before Pilate in the way that Moses eventually will appear before Pharaoh. It is Jesus who brings consternation and bewilderment on the empire, because he embodies and enacts the truth that will not be contained in imperial categories. This Jesus is the human bearer of truth that refuses to conform to power.
- Fourth there is *the God of truth* who confounds Pilate in the way that the God of truth confounded the power of Pharaoh. The agency of God is understated in this narrative of Jesus (in contrast to the exodus story) but is nonetheless clearly decisive. In response to Pilate, Jesus answers, "My kingdom is not from here" (John 18:36).

     He challenges the power of the governor by saying: "You would have no power over me unless it had been given you from above" (19:11).

The two phrases, "from here" and "from above," are subtle but forceful affirmations that there is another agency that is impinging on this narrative action, and that Pilate—the force of empire—is not a free autonomous agent as he imagines himself to be.

Both narratives—the exodus narrative of Israel and the trial narrative of Jesus—are told by the church, the first after the manner of the synagogue. It is the work of the church to tell these stories with all the characters being given their appropriate participation. Such a telling provides a map of power in the world and shows how that map of power is impinged on by the inexplicable force of truth. Pharaoh did not expect to be defeated by the power of the God whose name he did not know. And Pilate did not expect to be placed on trial as he presided over the trial of Jesus. Both stories insist that the world is not simplistic, domesticated, and one-dimensional as the empire imagines. And that is because among the indispensable characters in the world is the God who summons Moses and the God who gives power from above. This holy intentionality that courses through the narrative courses as well through our contemporary halls of power and our contemporary chambers of justice. In the service of that holy intention is a transformative human agent, first Moses and then Jesus. No amount of power in the world, it is attested, can hope to be valid or persuasive or effective until this full cast of characters is acknowledged and taken seriously.

THE PLOT OF THE EXODUS STORY

Given these characters, we may now line out *the plot* through which power and truth face each other. The exodus tale is an account of the way in which power is not free to disregard truth. For that reason, the plot turns on the ways that the agents of power never suspect or anticipate. Such truthfulness is, every time, a surprise in the environs of power. But that, of course, is why we engage with and persist with this story.

The plot begins with a public outburst of unbearable pain on the part of the peasants who have been reduced to slavery: "After a long time the king of Egypt died. The Israelites groaned under their slavery, and cried out" (Exod. 2:23).

The pain is caused by the imposition of the ruthless, demanding production schedules of Pharaoh. It has taken a very long time for the slaves to gather and muster a voice of protest. The sounding of that voice is risky; it is the risk run by every uncredentialed surfacing of the oppressed. It is the hazard undertaken by every whistle-blower in the corporation. It is the grievance of every abused person who finally will assert, "I am not going to take it anymore."

It is of immense importance that it is the breaking of the silence from below that initiates the narrative and that begins the historical process for Israel. The story does not begin with divine initiative, contrary to the Augustinian conviction that God takes all initiatives. Indeed, God is absent in the narrative until evoked by the cries of pain. This story begins wherever there is enough courage and freedom and daring and sensibility to acknowledge that the pain of ruthless exploitation is not normal and cannot be borne. Until that moment of utterance, every objective analysis of economic production in Egypt would have concluded that the pain of the peasants is a necessary, normal, even natural arrangement of labor—the cost of doing business. The shrillness of the cry constitutes an exposé of this normal as wholly abnormal and beyond bearing. Thus, in their utterance, the peasants-become-slaves:

- announce their presence as subjects and agents in history, not simply as objects of the economic system;
- refuse to be a silent, invisible participant in acquisitive production; and
- voice their bodily rage that was not taken seriously by anyone in Egypt who had power.

It is of strategic importance that the cry of the peasants-become-slaves is not addressed to anyone. The narrative does not say, "They cried out to . . . ." They just cried out! The sound is an eruption of bodily extremity that is now recognized and honored, no longer to be swallowed as per the requirements of the power system. The hinge of the plot of "power and truth" is in the next sentence: "Out of the slavery their cry for help rose up to God" (2:23).

They did not direct their cry in that way. They did not even dare to hope for a response. They knew only about the gods of the big house, and they had no hope of any of these gods hearing, because such well-fed gods have learned long ago not to heed the shrill noises that come from the labor pool (see Ps. 82:2–7). But this God is different, attests the plot. It is as though this God hovers around the places,

Where cross the crowded ways of life,
Where sound the cries of race and clan,
Above the noise of selfish is strife,
We hear Thy voice, O Son of Man.

In haunts of wretchedness and need
On shadowed thresholds fraught with fears,
From paths where hide the lures of greed,
We catch the vision of thy tears.[15]

It turns out, in the contest of power and truth, that this God is a magnet who draws pain to God's own self. The

narrative recharacterizes God so that now the pained slaves
engage the God who will triangle with them against Pharaoh so that the map of power and truth must be redrawn.
God is drawn into the power map of pain: "'I have heard
their cry on account of their taskmasters. Indeed, I know
their sufferings'" (Exod. 3:7).

God's response to the cry is a big self-assertion and a
big resolve to match the self-assertion. In an inscrutable
way, God meets Moses the fugitive in a direct, numinous
encounter, and God declares God's self to be the God who
had inhabited the book of Genesis with promises. In this
self-declaration, this God assures that the promises of the
book of Genesis are now operative in the book of Exodus,
only now they are addressed to a ragtag company of slaves.
It is as though this God is a sucker for voiced pain and cannot withhold full engagement with those who give voice in
such circumstance.

In Exodus 3:7–9, YHWH is a big, self-assertive talker.
God resolved:

I have seen their misery
I have heard their cry
I know their sufferings
I have come down to deliver
I will bring them to a good and broad land
For I have seen how the Egyptians oppress them

That divine declaration goes on for three wondrous verses!

But then, abruptly, YHWH ends the speech of self-
resolve. Suddenly, in verse 10 the rhetoric shifts as YHWH
says to Moses: And now, you go!

YHWH's resolve to counter the exploitation system of
Pharaoh is extended to human agency, specifically to this

fugitive from imperial power, this freedom-fighter/terrorist. The story pivots on the way in which divine resolve is transposed into human agency. So now, Moses becomes the carrier, agent, and witness to revelatory truth that challenges established, absolute power. Thus the narrative cunningly links *holy intention* and *human agency* in a way that anticipates, for Christians, the enigmatic formula: two natures in one person, two resolves in one agent. The outcome of the narrative mandate given by YHWH to Moses is that none can misconstrue the initiative of Moses as a one-dimensional human enterprise. The outcome is a new contestation about power that had long been perceived by all parties as absolute and beyond challenge.

From this moment on, Pharaoh is no longer free to define and dictate the terms of social power and the nature of social relationships. Pharaoh is effectively checked in his power by Moses' enactment of bodily truth that carries the current of the God of Genesis. The divine mandate given the human agent is elemental: "So come, I will send you to Pharaoh to bring my people, the Israelites, out of Egypt" (3:10).

Afterward, Moses and Aaron went to Pharaoh and said, "Thus says the LORD, the God of Israel, 'Let my people go, so that they may celebrate a festival to me in the wilderness'" (5:1).

All parties understand that the purpose of stating "celebrate a festival to me in the wilderness" (outside the territory over which Pharaoh presides) is a dramatic shift of loyalty and energy that amounts to nothing less than a liturgical drama of rejecting and dethroning the power of Pharaoh. It is known already, then, that the subversive liturgy directed toward an alternative God is an immediate threat to established power. This is a reality known by the killers of Archbishop Romero and by the white power elite who watched Martin and his companions kneel and pray in the street, a drama of "overcoming."

Pharaoh's response to YHWH's mandate is terse: "'Who is YHWH that I should heed him and let Israel go? I do not know the LORD, and I will not let Israel go'" (5:2, au. trans.).

In fact, Pharaoh mockingly said, "Yeah. . . who?!" I do not know the name. I do not acknowledge that authority. Pharaoh is at deep risk—and knows that he is at deep risk— by the bodily truthfulness carried by this reluctant human agent.

PHARAOH'S POWER CONTESTED

Thus power is contested. It is contested through the extended drama of the plagues that are not to be explained away as natural phenomena (Exod. 6–11). They are exhibits of awesome divine power and resolve before which the power of Pharaoh is helpless.

After the river is turned to blood (7:14–25) and after the frogs (8:1–15), the third round of the contest concerns gnats. After the two rounds of contested power that ended in a draw, in the third try the Egyptian technicians (the roster of learned men in and of the empire) could not match the power of YHWH: They could not! (8:18). They are not able! The power of Pharaoh has reached its limit in a dramatic way. Pharaonic power does not run as far as YHWH's power enacted by Moses and Aaron. (The failure on gnats is like not having an atomic bomb, thus a poor competitor in the big race.) After that, it is a mop-up action for YHWH, with Pharaoh making a reluctant, grudging retreat before the saving power of YHWH-cum-Moses.

By Exodus 8:25, Pharaoh knows that he must compromise because his power is not absolute any longer. He is prepared to let the slaves "sacrifice to your God," but "within the land," that is, under supervision and surveillance. When Moss refuses that grudging offer, Pharaoh grants a permit to go into the wilderness, but not "very far away" (8:28). And then, Pharaoh petitions Moses, "'Pray for me'" (8:28). The narrative permits Pharaoh a slight dawning about the new, changed world he must now inhabit in which he must yield small bits of power. His conduct is the usual way of an overthrown dictator who always catches on slowly about the new flow of power and who always makes small concessions without recognizing that the game is in fact over.

By 10:8, Pharaoh concedes that some may leave to worship YHWH, that is, to change loyalties, but then he asks as a ploy, "'But which ones are to go?'"

It is as though the tyrant allows a quota to depart and then requires the leader to select who will go and who must remain. And we know, from the death camps in Germany, about selection. Of course Moses refuses and declares that none will go until all go—an anticipation of the way in which Nelson Mandela refused the chance to depart prison early without his companions.

By 10:24, Pharaoh wants to hold only the flocks and herds of Israel as surety:

"Go, worship the LORD. Only your flocks and your herds shall remain behind. Even your children may go with you." (10:24)

Moses again refuses: "'Not a hoof will be left behind'" (v. 26). Moses knows that the tide has turned, and he has no need to compromise with Pharaoh.

Pharaoh twice concedes that he has sinned:

> "This time I have sinned; the LORD is in the right, and I and
> my people are in the wrong. Pray to the LORD. Enough of
> God's thunder and hail! I will let you go; you need stay no
> longer." (9:27–28)

> "I have sinned against the LORD your God, and against
> you. Do forgive my sin just this once, and pray to the LORD
> your God that at the least he remove this deadly thing from
> me." (10:16–17)

Pharaoh now knows! But he cannot bring himself to face
the fact that the truth of the slaves-cum-YHWH has undone
his shaky claim to power and has negated whatever legitimacy he may have once had. The confession and the prayer
of Pharaoh constitute an acknowledgment of YHWH, but
Moses takes them to be strategic ploys rather than authentic
recognition. And so Moses responds yet again:

> "As soon as I have gone out of the city, I will stretch out my
> hands to the LORD; the thunder will cease, and there will
> be no more hail, so that you may know that the earth is the
> LORD's" (9:29)

Pharaoh must know fully, must acknowledge, must concede,
must yield.[16]

And indeed, by 10:7 Pharaoh is the only one left who
will not yield. His most trusted advisers know better:

> Pharaoh's officials said to him, "How long shall this fellow
> be a snare to us? Let the people go, so that they may wor-
> ship the LORD their God; do you not yet understand that
> Egypt is ruined?"

This counsel to the king is not unlike the way in which the
advisers to Lyndon Johnson all knew that the war in Vietnam was lost and now could only destroy what was left of

Johnson's political legacy. So it was with Pharaoh. His policy of resistance left Pharaoh and his regime in shambles. But such raw power that imagines itself to be absolute never learns in time.

In the concluding scene of this drama, Pharaoh, now of necessity alert to the emancipatory truth of YHWH, summons Moses and says to him:

> "Rise up, go away from my people, both you and the Israelites! Go, worship the LORD, as you said. Take your flocks and your herds, as you said, and be gone." (12:31–32)

Power must now acknowledge *truth.* The truth that meets power here is the combination of attentive *divine resolve* and the *bodily assertion* of the slaves who suffer out loud. Pharaoh, the last to catch on, now knows that his exploitative power has no future. Indeed, by the end he knows even more than that; he knows about "the migration of the holy."[17] God's holiness has departed Egypt and has settled on this company of shrill, demanding, enraged slaves. And so he says in his last utterance in this dramatic narrative: "And bring a blessing on me too!" (12:32).

In this utterance we have the great Egyptian embodiment of worldly power on its knees, in supplication, asking that the power for life from God, that is "blessing," be given by this fugitive who carries radical public truth that is effective transformative power. This climactic utterance is breathtaking in its recognition that the locus of power has shifted; holiness is allied with unbearable human pain now brought to speech and to active power.[18]

A final comment on this narrative encounter. As you know, the text is not reportage; it is, rather, critical reflection based on memory at some distance from what may have happened. The narrators characterize this self-conscious interpretive intentionality in 10:1–2. Pharaoh operated with a hard heart, that is, he conceded and retracted and conceded and retracted. He did so, they say, in order to keep the story going. And the reason to keep the story going episode after episode is,

> in order that I may show these signs of mine among them, and that you may tell your children and grandchildren how I made fools of the Egyptians and what signs I have done among them—so that you may know that I am the LORD.

The purpose is to attest the power of YHWH as player in the public drama. More than that, the purpose is to tell the grandchildren. This is a teaching curriculum in a narrative form so that you and your grandchildren, unlike Pharaoh, will learn to know YHWH in time. The intent is that you will recognize that the map of power and truth is complex and multidimensional. The story is reiterated in order that the coming generation should not be seduced by Pharaoh's simplistic reading of power that is impervious to the transformative potential of social pain when it is enacted in the public domain.

THE EXODUS STORY: READING AS CONTESTANTS

Because we ourselves are the instructed, socialized grandchildren of these narratives, we keep reading this odd testimony. Indeed, we keep reading it for all its poignant contemporaneity, even while we recognize that it is only a story. It is not a doctrine or a proposition or a proof; we do not even know what history stands behind the story. We do not, we know, need to take the narrative too seriously, because it is not more than a story. Nevertheless, when we read attentively we find ourselves taken with its profound gravitas. Reading in this way, we ask about transposing the old narrative into present reality. We ask about the four characters and we ask about the plot that continues to be reperformed before our very eyes. We ask:

1. Who plays the pharaoh in our current performance of the drama, the one who acts in anti-neighborly, exploitative ways and operates a political-economic system that is organized for greedy acquisitiveness?
2. Where are the cries from exhausted laborers who, in their exhaustion, break the silence because their bodies will no longer lie?
3. Where is the holy power of God operative in ways that subvert or jeopardize established power in the interest of the aggrieved?
4. Who are the human agents who carry holy alternatives that are intended by the Lord of emancipation?

We notice, as we risk offering answers to these questions, that the map of social power is, as always, dislocated by the truth when pain and holiness collude in subversion. We notice, given such a map of destabilized social power, that the drama is always again *revolutionary* in its potential and at the same time *revelatory* of purposes that are beyond our systems of control. The interface of *revolutionary and revelatory* is characteristic of this plot and always awaits fresh performance.

As we engage that plot and entertain the notion of its fresh reperformance, we see the outcome of the original performance:

- They tore themselves away from Pharaoh's system, even though they later recalled that his system assured a steady stream of food (see Num. 11:4–6).
- They went through the deep waters of risk where Pharaoh and his enforcers could not follow.
- They came out on the other side and danced for the first time, their emancipated bodies now free of brick quotas, unencumbered by the requirements of Pharaoh. Thus Moses sang: "The Lord will reign forever and ever" (Exod. 15:18).
- And Miriam and the other emancipated women sang and danced: "Sing to the LORD, for he has triumphed gloriously; horse and rider he has thrown into the sea" (15:21).

They are on their way, beyond the waters, through the desert, toward a new covenantal shaping of life at Sinai. The sequence of the plot makes clear, and continues to make clear, that the possibility of emancipation for covenantal alternative requires a departure (exodus!) from the way the world conventionally maps power. That conventional mapping of power does not take into account the collusion of holy resolve and human cry, a combination that Pharaoh found, eventually, to be irresistible.

So we dare to imagine the church:

1. Sounding the cry
2. Contesting for the alternative
3. Acting out the alternative
4. Dancing out beyond slavery

This is a narrative that we keep reperforming as we have the courage to do so. We are, for the most part, timid and inured in Pharaoh's narrative. His system has such a grip on us that we stay fixed on the endless quotas of exploitation, quotas of production and consumption. That fix is evident even in the disciples of Jesus. Mark reports of them: "'They did not understand about the loaves, but their hearts were hardened'" (Mark 6:52).

The reference to hard hearts means that the disciples thought like Pharaoh, who had the quintessential hard heart. They, like Pharaoh, thought in terms of acquisitiveness, anxiety, and self-security. The result is that they could not understand about the abundant bread given by the God of emancipation. They are so caught in that old ideology of power that they missed so much of the truth of distributive grace that was enacted in the old manna narrative and that is reiterated in the gospel of Jesus. It is no wonder that the narrative is always reperformed yet again, in order that we may recognize that recurring bondage among us and entertain that the departure from that bondage of one-dimensional power in response to the emancipatory truth is triggered by the cries of the oppressed.

NOTES

1. See Michael Walzer, *Exodus and Revolution* (New York: Basic Books, 1985).
2. Hans Walter Wolff, "The Hermeneutics of the Old Testament," in *Essays on Old Testament Hermeneutics,* ed. Claus Westermann, trans. James Luther Mays (Richmond, VA: John Knox Press, 1963) has written of the function of the Old Testament in Christian faith:

We must understand that the unspeakable gift in Christ is all too quickly misunderstood as spiritual, individualistic, and transcendental, if we do not hold before our eyes its original in the covenant Yahweh granted to Israel. He who gives himself to his community through forgiveness of sins in his death and his Resurrection, so that he is forever Lord and Shepherd, is also concerned with giving gifts for and directing its temporal life in the world (179).

Wolff then offers four theses about the function of the Old Testament in Christian faith:

- This is the way in which the Old Testament text must continue to speak with its characteristic witness, just in order to show the Christ-event as an eschatological act of God, and guard against false isolation and historization. (191)
- The Old Testament prevents the witness to Christ from being corrupted into philosophy about Christ. (194)
- The Old Testament guards the Christian message from false individualizing. (196)
- The Old Testament keeps the Christian message from transcendentalism. (198)

3. See Gary Dorrien, "No Common Good?" *Christian Century* 128, no. 8 (April 19, 2011): 22–25.

4. William T. Cavanaugh, *Migrations of the Holy: God, State, and the Political Meaning of the Church* (Grand Rapids: Eerdmans, 2011) offers a compelling statement about the political role of the church in the public world.

5. On the agenda of neighborliness, see John McKnight and Peter Block, *The Abundant Community: Awakening the Power of Families and Neighborhoods* (San Francisco: Berrett-Koehler, 2010).

6. Paul Lehmann, *The Transfiguration of Politics: The Presence and Power of Jesus of Nazareth in and over Human Affairs* (New York: Harper & Row, 1975), 48–70.

7. Ibid., 53.

8. See John Bright, *A History of Israel,* 4th ed. (Louisville, KY: Westminster John Knox Press, 2000), 120–24.

9. I take the generative phrase from James Boyd White, *Living Speech: Resisting the Empire of Force* (Princeton, NJ: Princeton University Press, 2006).

10. The quotation "food is a weapon" is attributed to Maxim Litvinov, former Soviet Commissar of Foreign Affairs during the 1930's famine in the Ukraine, and it was printed on posters in the United States to promote food conservation during World War II. Earl Butts, U.S. Secretary of Agriculture during the 1970s, also repeated this phrase.

11. Barbara Green, "The Determination of Pharaoh: His Characterization in the Joseph Narrative (Genesis 37–50)," in *The World of Genesis: Persons, Places, Perspectives,* ed. Philip R. Davies and David J. A. Clines (*JSOT* Supp. 257; Sheffield: Sheffield Academic Press, 1998), 150–77, has most fully and cunningly exposited the dramatic way in which the narrative minimizes Pharaoh and enhances the rule of YHWH.

12. See R. W. L. Moberly, *The Old Testament of the Old Testament: Patriarchal Narratives and Mosaic Yahwism* (OBT; Minneapolis: Fortress Press, 1992).

13. Leon Kass, *The Beginning of Wisdom: Reading Genesis* (New York: Free Press, 2003), 569 and *passim.*

14. On Moses as emancipator, see Aaron Wildavsky, *The Nursing Father: Moses as a Political Leader* (Tuscaloosa: University of Alabama Press, 1984); and Bruce Feiler, *America's Prophet: Moses and the American Story* (New York: William Morrow, 2009).

15. *The Presbyterian Hymnal* (Louisville, KY: Westminster John Knox Press, 1990), no. 408.

16. Note should be taken of Isaiah 19:21–22 that comes very late in the Old Testament and anticipates Egypt's full and positive engagement with YHWH:

> The LORD will make himself known to the Egyptians; and the Egyptians will know the LORD on that day, and will worship with sacrifice and burnt offering, and they will make vows to the LORD and perform them. The LORD will strike Egypt, striking and healing; they will return to the LORD, and he will listen to their supplications and heal them.

17. In *Migrations of the Holy,* Cavanaugh traces the way in which the "glory of the Lord" in the early modern period moved from the church to the nation states. In my use of the term from Cavanaugh,

I suggest that in the exodus narrative the movement was in the other direction, away from the kingdom of Pharaoh to the community of YHWH.

18. Walzer, *Exodus and Revolution,* 149, concludes his study with this sentence: "There is no way to get from here to there except by joining together and marching."

Chapter 2

VISIBLE POWER, TRUTH CUNNINGLY SUBVERSIVE

Solomon

THE SUBJECT OF SOLOMON IS BOUND TO COME UP WHEN WE THINK about power in the Old Testament. Solomon is remembered in the text as the apex of power in ancient Israel, for he stood at the center of what must have been a global economy.

SOLOMON'S DESTINY OF *SHALOM*

In the primary narrative we have Solomon. He is presented as YHWH's man of destiny, grounded in the promises of David, schooled in the arts of government, intimate with YHWH, held in awe by his entourage, and highly esteemed by his neighboring counterpart rulers (1 Kgs. 3–11).

He was born to David and Bathsheba, the son of promise after their son conceived in adultery had died (2 Sam. 12:15–23, 24–25). He is named Jedidiah, "beloved of the

Lord." The name bespeaks the hope that Solomon, like his father, David, would enjoy the special treatment and preferential regard of YHWH.

His throne name, evidently, is Solomon, a name linked to the term *shalom*. Thus he is identified as the carrier of *shalom*, the bringer of wholeness, peace, and well-being to his realm.

He rules in Jeru-*shalom*, the city anciently remembered as *Salem*, that is, *shalom* (Gen. 14:18). That ancient naming links the city to Abram and to the creator God who would preside over the cosmos-sustaining temple in Jerusalem:

> "Blessed be Abram by God Most High,
> maker of heaven and earth;
> and blessed be God Most High,
> who has delivered your enemies into your hand!"
> (Gen. 14:19–20)

It is plausible that this remembered doxology was situated in that religious sanctuary, so that Solomon's temple anthem is heir and echo of that ancient song (see 1 Kgs. 8:12–13).

Solomon, the bearer of *shalom* in Jeru-*salem*, is liturgically certified to establish a *pax Jerusalem*, a new world order of peace and prosperity. As is usual with such ambitious undertakings, the unspoken side of such ambitious peace and prosperity is that the dynasty and royal city are to be on the receiving end of the produce and revenue of the global economy. Thus, on all counts Solomon occupies center stage in ancient Israel's imagination as it ponders effective worldly power that is to be visible in political and economic terms. By any common reasoning, Solomon is the good king who effectively transformed a modest hill country people with a peasant economy into a much noticed regional, if not global, presence.

SOLOMON'S SUCCESSES

That presentation of Solomon that clusters around a destiny of *shalom,* in ancient articulation, is matched by our own popular remembrance when the biblical tradition is read with trusting innocence. Thus in popular rendering, most especially in the teaching of the church but more broadly in unreflective cultural assumption as well, Solomon is remembered as a huge success.

On the one hand, he is esteemed for the building of the temple, a grand exhibit of wealth and craftsmanship that came to be an appropriate way in which to house YHWH's own glory and presence (see 1 Kgs. 8:12–13 cited above). The temple of Solomon is so compelling in artistic imagination that we have been kept busy pondering modern viable replicas of it. There can be no doubt that the attachment of the Masonic Order to Solomon and to Solomon's temple and to Solomon's masons has advanced the popular notion of the temple.[1] In the eighteenth century, Masons proposed a nonsectarian, communal religion that would supersede the lethal sectarianism of Europe, and we can see that Solomon's temple was an appropriate icon for the order because Solomon's temple attempted to transcend sectarian truth and any embarrassing particularity that marked Israel's earlier tradition. Thus Solomon's temple has functioned in modern interpretation as a noble religious exhibit that moved beyond old disputatious rivalries.[2]

On the other hand, Solomon enjoys a reputation for wisdom, a reputation that is largely based on the folk narrative of 1 Kings 3:16–28 concerning the dispute between two mothers and a disputed child. The reported adjudication of Solomon evidences a worldly wisdom about the passion of mother-love and the cynical courage of the king to go for broke with the seemingly ruthless command, "'Bring me a sword'" (1 Kgs. 3:24). The outcome discloses Solomon's capacity to see through the subterfuge of the non-mother in order to arrive at a compelling and just verdict. It is no wonder that the narrative account ends in a great affirmation:

> All Israel heard of the judgment that the king had rendered; and they stood in awe of the king, because they perceived that the wisdom of God was in him, to execute justice. (1 Kgs. 3:28)

Solomon is presented as a practitioner of wisdom in the service of justice.

The combination of *temple-building* and *wisdom* generated, in common assumption, the success of the predestined king of *shalom*. The consequence is a ruler of wealth and power and splendor who has the whole world at his feet:

> Thus King Solomon excelled all the kings of the earth in riches and in wisdom. The whole earth sought the presence of Solomon to hear his wisdom, which God had put into his mind. Every one of them brought a present, objects of silver and gold, garments, weaponry, spices, horses, and mules, so much year by year. (1 Kgs. 10:23–25)

In the narrative account, that whole world is represented and embodied by the Queen of Sheba; she should have been his rival and competitor, but she is in fact completely overwhelmed by Solomon in his splendor. The usual rendering of 1 Kings 10:5 is: "There was no more spirit in her." The term *spirit* (*ruah*) also may be *breath*, so that we might read, "He took her breath away." Solomon is presented as the ancient ruler who took away their breath. And in popular, even contemporary imagination, the same response pertains. His temple, his wisdom, and his splendor do indeed take one's breath away, so awed are we by his achievements.

LOOKING FOR TRUTH BENEATH POWER

If, however, we are to consider the *power of Solomon* in the *context of truth*, we are not permitted to read too innocently. We may not take at face value either the ancient imagination of Solomon or the modern popular sense we have of him. We know enough, in our own contemporary context, to be suspicious of every new world order because such an effort is never innocent or disinterested; it is always, to some important extent, a front for self-interest perpetrated through violence. We have seen enough through the twentieth century of rapacious ideologies and posturing rulers in their strutting absolutism not to accept such posturing at face value. It is, of course, a tricky business with the Bible, as we are wont, contemporarily and popularly, to read it innocently. We can nevertheless readily recognize that Solomon, as he is imagined in the text, faced a prospect of power, prosperity, and success that was not only an enormous possibility for a peaceable order, given the power vacuum in his region. He also faced a prospect that was an enormous temptation to ambition and self-advancement. The sloganeering of his ancient interpreters posits an enormous seduction for Solomon, his entourage, and his legacy.

The danger for them (and for us) is to believe the press notices that fly atop the facts on the ground. Thus a discerning reader who asks about how truth impinges on power does not incline to take the reports of power at face value but seeks to look beneath for hints of truth that jeopardize such blanket claims of power. We are aware that the Solomon text of 1 Kings 3–11 is not simply reportage, but it is an artistic act of interpretive imagination.[3] As a result, we will be aware that there is something going on in the text other than what we read at face value, a more subtle and complex testimony to the legacy of the great king.

In order to sense the subtlety of the text we will watch for hints of irony in the literary presentation. Carolyn Sharp has especially noticed the "intersection of irony and royal power in Hebrew Bible texts."[4] Her own interest is in foreign rulers who are treated so that biblical authors could satirize dangerous systems of power. There is no doubt, however, that such dangerous systems of power were known not only outside Israel but inside Israel as well, most especially in the rule of Solomon. Wayne Booth has written more broadly of the "secret communion" between author and reader.[5] He might well have said "collusion," whereby the author writes beneath the surface and the reader "gets it." Thus author and reader collude to communicate with each other below the surface about royal power, not impressed by either the force of ancient popular imagination or the mantras of modern popular reading. Thus it is a doublespeak for which the alert reader is vigilant.[6] Our theme of power and truth brings to the fore in the Solomon narrative very little direct articulation of abrasive truth, perhaps because the narrative is so compelling and uncompromising in its celebration of Solomon. As a result, the force of truth in the narrative is characteristically, and perhaps of necessity, more indirect and discrete. But it is not, for that reason, any less powerful or important. In what follows, we may attempt to read knowingly about truth and power. I will in turn attend to

- How Solomon came to power
- How he kept and practiced power
- How he lost power

SOLOMON'S RISE TO POWER

Solomon's *rise to power* receives a good deal of attention in the narrative, as though his rise were a textbook example of the practice of power. The crisis of governance and the opportunity for Solomon occur because aging David, his father the king, could no longer maintain a vitality (1 Kgs. 1:1). Solomon is immediately plunged into the rough and tumble of family politics, competing with his brother, Adonijah, for the throne. It was not obvious that Solomon would rule after David, and the palace circles were choosing up sides for a hard-ball contest to come (1 Kgs. 1:7–8). Solomon came to power through vigorous, aggressive contestation.

Solomon's arrival on the throne was through a carefully choreographed subterfuge, designed to deceive the old king and mobilize him on behalf of his ambitious son. The agents of the act were Solomon's mother, Bathsheba (see 1 Kgs. 12:14), and Nathan, the court prophet (see 1 Kgs. 1:8). The narrative traces the plot in detail.

First, Nathan, vigilant for his own power, goes to Bathsheba and gives her the orchestrated lines she is to speak to the old king:

> Go in at once to King David and say to him, "Did you not, my lord the king, swear to your servant, saying, Your son Solomon shall succeed me as king and he shall sit on my throne? Why then is Adonijah king?" (1:13)

Nathan has an acute sense of effective timing: "Then while you are still there speaking with the king, I will come in after you and confirm your words" (1:14).

Bathsheba dutifully performs the lines assigned her by Nathan and fills out her role with other words:

> "My lord, you swore to your servant by the LORD your God saying: Your son Solomon shall succeed me as king, and he shall sit on my throne. But now suddenly Adonijah has become king, though you, my lord the king, do not know it. He has sacrificed oxen, fatted cattle, and sheep in abundance, and has invited all the children of the king, the priest Abiathar, and Joab the commander of the army, but your servant Solomon he has not invited. But you, my lord the king—the eyes of all Israel are on you to tell them who shall sit on the throne of my lord the king after him. Otherwise it will come to pass, when my lord the king sleeps with his ancestors, that my son Solomon and I will be counted offenders." (vv. 17–21)

Nathan follows through, as he promised, to reinforce the initiative of Bathsheba:

> While she was still speaking with the king, the prophet Nathan came in. The king was told, "here is the prophet Nathan." When he came in before the king, he did obeisance to the king, with his face to the ground. Nathan said, "My lord the king, Have you said, 'Adonijah shall succeed me as king, for he shall sit on my throne?' . . . Has this thing been brought about by my lord the king and you have not let your servant know who should sit on the throne of my lord the king after him?" (vv. 22–24, 27)

Nathan's instruction and subsequent speech reflect the same careful design: "still speaking" (vv. 14, 22) with the entire accent on the oft-repeated, "my lord the king," a formula much used in order to flatter, seduce, and manipulate the old king.

The scheme works! The old king, now duly manipulated and instructed, gives the verdict the drama was designed to evoke:

> "As the Lord lives, who has saved my life from every adversary, as I swore to you by the Lord, the God of Israel, 'Your son Solomon shall succeed me as king, and he shall sit on my throne in my place' so will I do this day." (vv. 29–30)

The dramatic performance concludes with the mantra of Bathsheba, a doublespeak that salutes the old king while at the same time verifying her own declaration: "'May my lord King David live forever'" (v. 31). The formula is a curiosity in this context, if not a blatant contradiction. It is precisely her hope that the old king will not live very long at all.

David follows through with a command that intends to legitimate Solomon:

> "There let the priest Zadok and the prophet Nathan anoint him king over Israel; then blow the trumpet, and say, 'Long live King Solomon!' You shall go up following him. Let him enter and sit on my throne; he shall be king in my place; for I have appointed him to be ruler over Israel and over Judah." (vv. 34–35)

The narrative provides a carefully designed series of speeches that move effectively to the proper conclusion. We notice that the narrator who reports this action is in the background and offers no evaluative or interpretive comment. The words speak for themselves; but the sum of the words is that the Davidic appointment of Solomon is one of deception, not of legitimacy. David's gift to Solomon is completely arbitrary, at the behest of his cunning, duplicitous companions.

Power, Deception, and Violence

The achievement through *deception* is followed by consolidation through *violence*. One outcome of Solomon's arrival on the throne is that his brother, Adonijah, is fearful (1:50). Solomon offers his brother, his recent rival, a tentative, provisional reprieve: *"If* he proves to be a worthy man, not one of his hairs shall fall to the ground; but *if* wickedness is found in him, he shall die" (1:52). In fact, the new king lets the fate of his brother hang in the air, unresolved, with the double "if" of ominous conditionality.

In chapter 2, Solomon is given advice by his aged, feeble father. The juxtaposition of verses 1–4 and verses 5–9 is itself a huge irony. The first verses on the lips of his father concern Torah obedience. The second set of verses urge acts of violence that will secure the throne. We are, perhaps intended (perhaps not intended?) to notice the incongruity between David's two utterances. In verses 5–9, David identifies two enemies of Solomon who are potential threats to be eliminated. First concerning Joab: "Act therefore according to your wisdom, but do not let his gray head go down to Sheol in peace" (2:6).

Then, after a positive verse for Barzillai who had aided the royal house and to whom generosity is permitted (v. 7), the old man gives advice concerning Shemei: "Therefore do not hold him guiltless, for you are a wise man; you will know what you ought to do to him, and you must bring his gray head down with blood to Sheol" (v. 9).

In both of these cases, David links royal wisdom to a necessary killing: "according to your wisdom" (v. 6) and "you are a wise man" (v. 9). The appeal to wisdom, however, does not conceal the ruthless necessity of violent elimination. This is, of course, a very different wisdom from the lively folk tale of chapter 3 whereby Solomon secured his popular reputation for wisdom. Now wisdom is the will to do what is necessary to secure the throne, thus the necessity of violence. The mandate of the father is enacted by the son (vv. 13–46). The repeated, stylized formula of execution is a dramatic anticipation of the wholesale killing in *The Godfather,* wherein enemies are systematically eliminated, even while a veneer of propriety is maintained.

Adonijah commits an act of sheer foolishness that amounts to a challenge to his brother that cannot be disregarded and that offers a pretext for his murder. The desire to have the concubines of his father is a blatant act of defiance, and we may wonder about the risk that Adonijah was willing to run (2:15–18).[7] Except that Bathsheba is in the middle of the request—a fact that permits us to wonder if Adonijah is being framed in order to write his own death warrant (v. 19–24)—we cannot know.

Whether genuine or contrived, the initiative works as Bathsheba would have wanted it to work. The new king is enraged:

> "And why do you ask Abishag the Shunammite for Adonijah? Ask for him the kingdom as well! For he is my elder brother; ask not only for him but also for the priest Abiathar and for Joab son of Zeriah." Then King Solomon swore by the LORD, "So may God do to me, and more also, for Adonijah has devised this scheme at the risk of his life! Now therefore as the LORD lives, who has established me and placed me on the throne of my father David, and who has made me a house as he promised, today Adonijah shall be put to death." (vv. 22–24)

Perhaps this is a request by Adonijah; perhaps it is conjured by Bathsheba as a pretext. Solomon now has the evidence needed for the double "if" of 1:52, and so the execution follows: "So King Solomon sent Benaiah, son of Jehoiada; he struck him down, and he died" (v. 25).

The actual report of the killing is terse, as if we can almost hear in the narrative line the fall of the sword on the neck of the rival. The reprieve given to Abiathar the priest is conditional (2:26–27):

> "For you deserve death. But I will not at this time put you to death, because you carried the ark of the Lord God before my father David, and because you shared in all the hardships my father endured." (v. 26)

The generosity of the king toward the priest is "at this time," without any guarantee, of course, depending on the same "if" as uttered over Adonijah in 1:52.

The elimination of Joab is according to the direction of David (2:28–33; see 2:5–6). The act of execution reiterates the terse report of verse 25: "Then Benaiah son of Jehoiada went up and struck him down and killed him; and he has buried at his own house near the wilderness" (v. 34). We notice that in verse 35 Benaiah, for his bloody fidelity as Solomon's hit man, receives a military promotion. This is the same Benaiah who first said "Amen" to the new king in 1:36.

The execution of Shemei again follows the instruction of David (2:36–45; see 2:8–9). By now we know the cadence of the report of the killing: "Then the king commanded Benaiah son of Jehoiada; and he went out and struck him down, and he died" (v. 46).

In rapid succession, like a carefully implemented plan, Adonijah, Job, and Shemei are gone! And Abiathar is suspended according to the whim of the king. For good reason the narrative confirms the effectiveness of Solomon's combination of cunning and ruthlessness in laconic fashion: "So the kingdom was established in the hand of Solomon" (v. 46).

The establishment is accomplished by *deception and violence,* the twins of unfettered power. But a throne cannot be sustained finally by only deception and violence. It requires, eventually, more *legitimacy* than that. That legitimacy is enacted through the required royal liturgical performance: a Gihon (3:3–4). The liturgical performance is supplemented by the well-known dream of the king who dreamed of being a responsible, obedient ruler. The dream report concerns what is asked and what is given. In the asking, the king prays in all humility: "'Give your servant therefore an understanding mind to govern your people, able to discern between good and evil; for who can govern this your great people?'" (3:9).

What Solomon received, however, outran his asking because God is impressed with his modesty:

> "Because you have asked this, and have not asked for yourself long life or riches, or for the life of your enemies, but have asked for yourself understanding to discern what is right, I now do according to your word. Indeed I give you a wise and discerning mind; no one like you has been before you and no one like you shall arise after you. I give you also what you have not asked, both riches and honor all your life; no other king shall compare with you." (3:11–13)

In popular reading, of course, we focus on this act of *legitimacy* but regularly ignore the dramatic *deception* and the unembarrassed *violence* of the narrative. These three narrative accents, however, come together as the story of

Solomon's arrival, and we cannot simply choose the one we like. When we consider the three accents in sequence, we may say that we simply have conventional royal politics. What strikes one about the report is that the narrative does not comment on any of these aspects or make any judgment about them. Rather the narrative is permitted to have its full say, as though that is itself a conveyance of truth that presses itself on power. What we make of it depends on *how noble* we imagine the king to be. And that, in turn, depends on *how suspicious* we are as readers. Since we are considering power in the context of truth, we must ask about the way of truth in the text. Truth of a crucial, critical kind will recognize *deception* for what it is, and see that *violence* is in fact ruthlessly violent. And when deception and violence are recognized one will most probably be suspicious about the two acts of *legitimacy,* worship and dream. For surely the public performance of liturgy and the unverified report of the dream do not overcome the narrative specificity of deception and violence. At the very outset this is a celebration of power that we read with alertness and some disease, readily recognizing that we know enough to be suspicious of the surface presentation of the text and of our modern popularization of it. Power here is expressed as a not very pretty sight. As Reinhold Niebuhr has taught us, we are not permitted to be unthinkingly innocent about such power.[8]

SOLOMON'S PHARAONIC POWER

Solomon's retention and administration of power is offered as a narrative of great success. His reign was designed for peace and prosperity, or, more specifically, for the enhancement and aggrandizement of the king, for "no other king shall compare with you" (3:13). All parts of the royal system worked effectively to make Solomon staggeringly incomparable in the ancient world; in the remembered, imagined world of Israel; and in our popular celebration of him.

We are put on notice at the outset that Solomon's regime will be marked by ambiguity. In 3:3 we have it affirmed that "Solomon loved the Lord," that is, that he committed himself to the Torah covenant with YHWH; but in verse 1, just above, it is reported that Solomon married Pharaoh's daughter (see 7:8; 9:16, 24). The latter report means that he married into and committed to the mode of exploitative rule and abusive economics that Israel had already experienced from Pharaoh long before. The narrative proceeds without comment but no doubt with full awareness of the fact that Solomon's twin commitments—at the same time *to YHWH* and *to pharaonic rule*—are contradictory and mutually exclusive. It can be imagined that the report on Solomon's reign is a critical sorting out of these two commitments. Or given our theme of power and truth, we may say that the pharaonic marriage is the epitome of power and that love of YHWH is the dimension of truth in his narrative.

Over time Solomon gave himself increasingly to the practice of pharaonic power. The cry of the pharaonic system, already in Exodus 5, is *more*: more bricks, more labor, more exploitation of labor, all in response to the nightmare of scarcity.[9] Now, it appears, Solomon is like his father-in-law and like his pharaonic wife in the pursuit of more. Thus the story of Solomon's reign is the story of accumulation, for raw, unrestrained power is always in the service of more, regardless of the political or economic system that is said to prevail. The drive for more is rooted in *anxiety*. The goal of more is *monopoly*. And the means of more is exploitative

production that readily shades over into *violence.* Thus the
sequence of anxiety, scarcity, accumulation, monopoly, and
violence constitutes the story of Pharaoh in the exodus narrative. The same sequence comes to the fore in the rule of
Solomon. And without undue overreaching, we are able
to observe the same sequence in the rapacious capitalist-
consumerist economy of our society. The report of accumulation by Solomon might be seen as celebration, especially
if the narrative reflects the mood of an erstwhile culture of
agrarian peasants who want to salute one of our own who
made it big. Thus Solomon's own father, David, was in fact
a desperate bandit, rooted in peasant culture, who led raids
against the economic establishment of his time:[10]

> Everyone who was in distress, and everyone who was in
> debt, and everyone who was discontented gathered to him;
> and he became captain over them. (1 Sam. 22:2)

But such a memory of the father is quickly overridden by
the success of the son who no longer wants that aspect of
his father remembered.

Thus the reported accumulation of Solomon may be
peasant gloating. Except that peasants do not characteristically gloat over the amassed property of their overlord, for
they know that such surplus wealth is a product of their
own unrewarded labor. It is more likely, for that reason, that
what may appear on the surface to be gloating over Solomon's success should be taken ironically. Such irony was
designed to expose the extravagant self-indulgence of the
royal entourage that is quite inappropriate in the midst of
peasant realism. Thus the reader may decide if the narrative of accumulation is to be read as congratulations or as
ironic exposé. If the narrative bespeaks only power, then

restrained power should be celebrated. But if the narrative tells of power in the context of the truth of the Torah God, whom Solomon is said to love and to whom he has sworn allegiance, then the gloat may be replaced by a sturdier critical perspective. Here, I suggest that we read the power of Solomon, that is his capacity to accumulate that produces monopoly, in the context of the critical truth of the Torah. In that context, the report on accumulation is clearly exposé and not congratulations.

Food

Solomon accumulated huge amounts of *food* to nourish (bribe?) the royal entourage, the ones who were "happy" with his rule (1 Kgs. 4:20): "Solomon's provision for one day was thirty cors of choice flour, and sixty cors of meal, ten fat oxen, and twenty pasture-fed cattle, one hundred sheep, besides deer, gazelles, roebucks, and fatted fowl" (4:22–23).

This extravagant daily menu was enough for a huge company of courtiers and yes-men who sustained his consolidation of power in Jerusalem. The accent in the list is on *meat*, a sign of great indulgence. By contrast the peasants ate meat rarely and certainly not every day (see Amos 6:4!). The menu suggests a "movable feast" for the urban elites (more feast than movable) that must have been given widespread coverage in a way that was sure to evoke resentment and resistance.

Taxation

The cost of such indulgent extravagance was enormous. In order to *finance* such indulgence, Solomon devised a carefully ordered Internal Revenue Service that is detailed in

4:7–19. The twelve tax districts were required, each in turn, to finance the entire government for one month in the year. It is to be noted in passing that among the IRS officers, surely coveted positions given to insiders, are Benabinadab, son-in-law to Solomon (4:11), and Ahimaaz, also a son-in-law to the king (4:15). Thus the tax collecting agency was an operation of the urban elites for the benefit of the urban elites. One may imagine that this revenue apparatus was, like every exploitative tax system, resented by the peasants.

Luxuries

Solomon's accumulation of food and money is matched by his accumulation of *artistic work*. "He composed three thousand proverbs, and his songs numbered a thousand and five" (4:32). It is more than likely that Solomon is a collector and not a generator of such artistic renderings. Most likely he, like many of the idle rich, collected art partly as investment, partly as celebration of cultural life, and partly in order to exhibit his civic engagement. Thus even his artistic bent, whatever it may have been, is quantified so that it is transposed into yet another commodity transaction.

Cheap Labor

Solomon accumulated a force of *cheap labor*. It was anticipated in 1 Samuel 8:11–13 that the king would institute a military draft to provide muscle for the regime. And now Solomon benefits from such labor that is surely a replica of the work force of his father-in-law, the pharaoh. The memory of Israel is unstable about the matter, perhaps because the grief and embarrassment about forced labor is acute in its recall of the past. On the one hand, Solomon's cheap labor included his own Israelite subjects:

> King Solomon conscripted forced labor out of all Israel; the levy numbered thirty thousand men. He sent them to Lebanon, ten thousand a month in shifts; they would be a month in the Lebanon and two months at home. Adoniram was in charge of forced labor. Solomon also had seventy thousand laborers and eighty thousand stonecutters in the hill country, besides Solomon's three thousand three hundred supervisors who were over the work, having charge of the people who did the work. (5:13–16)

That huge work force of conscripted labor was supervised by Adoniram (v. 14). Indeed, in the bureaucratic roster of 4:1–6, Adoniram is named as Secretary of Labor (4:6). That inventory of workers acknowledges that Solomon had a cabinet officer to supervise forced labor. And underneath Adoniram there were a huge number of supervisors, suggesting that the regime was purposeful and well-ordered in its projects (5:16).[11]

But the memory of Israel is perhaps nervous about the matter. Thus in 9:15, 22, the tradition is at pains to correct the report of 5:13–16: "But of the Israelites Solomon made no slaves" (9:22a).

Even given that correction, however, the tradition is still willing to make a concession:

> They were the soldiers, they were his officials, his commanders, his captains, and the commanders of his chariotry and cavalry. They were the chief officers who were over Solomon's work; five hundred fifty, who had charge of the people who carried on the work. (9:22b–23)

The latter qualification indicates, as with Adoniram, that the force of cheap labor was managed by those among

the royal entourage, not unlike the taskmasters and supervisors of the pharaoh in Exodus 5. The entire scheme con-
tributed to the wealth, effectiveness, prestige, and control of
Solomon's ambitious policies and programs.

Arms Trafficking

Solomon also accumulated enough *arms* to qualify as a
National Security State. His traffic in arms served, no doubt,
to maximize his own security force. (See the reference to
the fortress cities in 9:15.) Beyond that, his arms program
was clearly a commercial enterprise that brought him great
wealth:

> Solomon's import of horses was from Egypt and Kue,
> and the king's traders received them from Kue at a price.
> A chariot could be imported from Egypt for six hundred
> shekels of silver, and a horse for one hundred and fifty;
> so through the king's traders they were exported to all the
> kings of the Hittites and the kings of Aram. (10:28–29; see
> as well 9:21–28).

Apex of a Global Economy

The result of his policies of cheap labor, commerce, and traffic in arms placed Solomon at *the center and apex of a global
economy*. There clearly were no limits to his acquisitiveness:

> The weight of gold that came to Solomon in one year was
> six hundred sixty-six talents of gold, besides that which
> came from the traders and from the business of the mer-
> chants, and from all the kings of Arabia and the gover-
> nors of the land. King Solomon made two hundred large
> shields of beaten gold; six hundred shekels of gold went

into each shield. He made three hundred shields of beaten gold; three minas of gold went into each shield; and the king put them in the House of the Forest of Lebanon. The king also made a great ivory throne, and overlaid it with the finest gold. The throne had six steps. The top of the throne was rounded in the back, and on each side of the seat were arm rests and two lions standing beside the arm rests, while twelve lions were standing, one on each end of a step on the six steps. Nothing like it was ever made in any kingdom. All King Solomon's drinking vessels were of gold, and all the vessels of the House of the Forest of Lebanon were of pure gold; none were of silver—it was not considered as anything in the days of Solomon. For the king had a fleet of ships of Tarshish at sea with the fleet of Hiram. Once every three years the fleet of ships of Tarshish used to come bringing gold, silver, ivory, apes, and peacocks. (10:14–22)

This extravagant rhetoric shows the way in which Solomon is remembered as larger than life. He clearly was an organizational genius who had a keen eye and a strong arm for the endless accumulation of commodities.

Women

Finally among his commodities was his accumulation of women: "Among his wives were seven hundred princesses and three hundred concubines" (11:3).

Wendell Berry has shrewdly observed that the treatment of women and the management of land are usually equivalent in a social practice, so that if one is abused, so is the other. Clearly Solomon, in his compulsion to accumulate, treated women, like all else, as a valuable commodity. It is likely that this extravagant number of women represents not so much sexuality as it embodies a network of political treaties and military alliances that were sealed with the exchange of women. It is important that the women are princesses, suggesting that they arise from important political connection and server to enhance Solomon's network of global security.

Solomon's Temple

The capstone of Solomon's accumulation is the construction of *the temple* in Jerusalem. Like every king in that ancient world, temple construction is a show of piety. But, of course, temple construction is also a show of power and wealth, designed at the same time to magnify the God of the regime and to enhance the regime itself. Thus the temple becomes the ultimate expression of Solomon's compulsion to accumulate, for it is remembered as a dazzling exhibit of wealth:

> The interior of the inner sanctuary was twenty cubits long, twenty cubits wide, and twenty cubits high; he overlaid it with *pure gold*. He also overlaid the altar with cedar. Solomon overlaid the inside of the house with *pure gold*, then he drew chains of *gold* across, in front of the inner sanctuary, and overlaid it with *gold*. Next he overlaid the whole house with *gold*, in order that the whole house might be perfect; even the whole altar that belongs to the inner sanctuary he overlaid with *gold*. (6:20–22).

> So Solomon made all the vessels that were in the house of the LORD: the *golden* altar, the *golden* table for the bread of the Presence, the lampstands of *pure gold*, five on the south side and five on the north, in front of the inner sanctuary; the flowers, the lamps, and the tongs, of *gold*; the cups, snuffers, basins, dishes for incense, and fire pans, of *pure gold*; the sockets for the doors of the inner most part of the house, the most holy place, and for the doors of the nave of the temple, of *gold*. (7:48–50)

The frequent repetition of the term *gold* cannot be accidental or incidental. The temple is an epitome of the entire system of accumulation grounded in anxiety, aimed at monopoly, and accomplished by exploitation.

Nor can there be any doubt that the political purpose and physical appearance of the temple impinged on the theology assumed and practiced in the temple. The theological purpose of the temple was to house and contain the God of the regime, so that that God would be resident as patron and guarantor of the regime. The choral anthem at the dedication of the temple situates YHWH permanently in the temple:

> The Lord has said that he would dwell in thick darkness.
> I have built you an exalted house,
> a place for you to dwell in forever.
>
> (8:12–13)

The Songs of Zion that are sung in the temple hold YHWH as patron and guarantor of the holy city:

> God is our refuge and strength,
> a very present help in trouble.
>
> (Ps. 46:1)

> Let Mount Zion be glad,
> let the towns of Judah rejoice because of your judgments.
> Walk about Zion, go all around,
>   count its towers,
> consider well its ramparts,
>   go through its citadels,
> that you may tell the next generation,
>   that this is God,
> our God forever and ever.
> He will be our guide forever.
>
> (Ps. 48:11–14)

In Judah God is known,
    his name is great in Israel.
His abode has been established in Salem,
    his dwelling place in Zion.
There he broke the flashing arrows,
    the shield, the sword, and the weapons of war.
                                    (Ps. 76:1–3)

The liturgy serves to domesticate God. If we are suspicious enough, we can see that this God has become so domesticated that the living God has been reduced to a safe, predictable idol. This regime, like every regime of unrestrained power, requires a God who is an adored object but who cannot be a restless, active subject. In the end, it appears that Solomon has been able to liturgically and theologically do to YHWH what he has been able to do to everything else—reduce God to a *commodity*. The vision of *shalom* enacted by Solomon is one of power manifested as wealth and control in dazzling proportion. On the surface of the text, there is no truth-telling voice that might call the enterprise into question.

TRUTH CONFRONTS SOLOMON

However, the regime of Solomon, like every absolutizing regime, cannot be sustained. Thus, as Solomon came to power by *deception* and *violence* with a legitimating act of piety, and as he held power by aggressive *accumulation* with the *legitimacy* of temple piety, we may consider how it was, in the memory of Israel, that power that was immune to Torah truth could last in grandeur for very long. It could not, however, last in the end, because such power is not the last word. The collapse of the kingdom of Solomon is as dramatic as its rise. As the Roman governor learned as he stood before Jesus, the question of truth will eventually surface with dangerous power and authority.

Truth is a quite subdued voice in the Solomon narrative, so powerful, so successful, and so totalizing is the rule of the king. Indeed, there are no explicit voices in the narrative that summon to truth. But even in that wholesale domination by Solomon, truth will make a trace of an appearance, stealthily and surely at great risk. The risk would have been great in the actual time of Solomon because the king would not tolerate such subversion. But even in the subsequent traditioning process, such truth-telling ran the unwelcome risk of exposing as fraud and failure Israel's number one example of success.

Nevertheless the Torah truth-tellers (Deuteronomists) manage to leave their trace of conscious critique and warning that destabilized the power of the king. In 1 Kings 3:14, after God has promised Solomon riches and honor on an incomparable scale (v. 13), the truth of the matter sounds next: "*If* you will walk in my ways, keeping my statutes and my commandment, as your father David walked, *then* I will lengthen your life."

The truth is that Torah-keeping is the condition of well-being, say these truth-tellers. The "if" of conditionality that they speak is an echo of the defining conditional "if" of Moses in Exodus 19:5: "Now therefore *if* you obey my voice and keep my covenant, [*then*] you shall be my treasured possession out of all the peoples."

In 1 Kings 6:12, in the midst of the temple construction, we are surprised to hear a conditional "if," again with reference to the commandments:

Concerning this house that you are building, *if* you will walk in my statutes, obey my ordinances, and keep all my commandments by walking in them, *then* I will establish my promise with you, which I made to your father David.

And in Solomon's second dream, perhaps a contrived literary disruption in the narrative, the conditionality of power is made clear in a syllogistic way. In 9:4–7, we are given a double "if," positive and negative, followed by a double "then" of positive and negative consequence:

Positive condition: As for you, *if* you will walk before me, as David your father walked, with integrity of heart and uprightness, doing according to all that I have commanded you, and keeping my statutes and my ordinances (v. 4)

Positive consequence: *Then* I will establish your royal throne over Israel forever, as I promised your father David, saying, "There shall not fail you a successor to the throne of Israel" (v. 5).

Negative condition: *If* you turn aside from following me, you or your children, and do not keep my commandments and my statutes that I have set before you, but go and serve other gods and worship them (v. 6)

Negative consequence: *Then* I will cut off Israel from the land that I have given them; and this house that I have consecrated for my name I will cast out of my sight (v. 7).

The final part, the negative consequence is extended and open-ended because the truth-tellers speak with great passion to a royal ideology that they reject. This tight, symmetrical statement reflects the rigorous logic of covenantal blessing and curse in the tradition of Deuteronomy.

The capacity of the tradition to scatter these statements of conditionality through the narrative of the king is quite remarkable, and the alert reader cannot fail to notice their disruptive force. But even as we belated readers notice, there is no hint in the text itself that these warnings are to be taken seriously by the characters in the drama. That fact no doubt reflects a complex traditioning process in which the importance of the "if" likely came later. But whatever may have been the editorial process that brought them to speech, there can be no doubt that the covenantal-theological substance of the claim was important in ancient Israel, because Israel's root memory concerns emancipation from socio-economic-theological absolutism. This regime of absolute power, like every such regime, is impervious to such assertion. Of course! It always is! The practitioners of absolutism always learn late, much too late. Thus the witnesses to what de-absolutizes are there, but unheeded and unnoticed.

Judgment Is Passed on Solomon

The recurring "if" in the Solomon narrative comes to a forceful conclusion in 11:1–13. It turns out, in the horizon of this truth-telling rendition, that Solomon, in his long practice of accumulation, has not obeyed the Torah. And when the "if" of Torah is unheeded, the "then" of judgment is sure to be enacted. These verses are cast in a traditional prophetic "speech of judgment" that consists in an *indictment* (for violating Torah) and a judicial *sentence* (a sanction from God). The indictment is given as a narrative report in verses 1–8. That narrative report judges that Solomon's many marriages have compromised his

Israelite identity and his obedience of the commandments of Torah. Specifically Solomon served other gods and so violated the command of Sinai to exclusiveness. The narrative report is reinforced by the more cryptic verdict of verses 9–10:

> Then the LORD was angry with Solomon, because his heart had turned away from the LORD, the God of Israel, who had appeared to him twice, and had commanded him concerning this matter, that he should not follow other gods; but he did not observe what the LORD commanded.

The narrative and the direct verdict agree: the first commandment was violated by the king! But we should not read innocently about the violation of the commandment, as though it were a religious infraction. The violation is socio-economic and political concerning the accumulation of material commodities at the expense of the neighbor, reducing all to commodities. The sentence that follows is introduced by "therefore," with active verbs, twice "tear" and once "give": "I will surely *tear* the kingdom from you and *give* it to your servant. . . . I will *tear* it out of the hand of your son" (vv. 11, 12).

As the indictment is not simply religious, so the threat need not be read as supernatural intervention. As we will see in what follows, the narrators understood very well that the tearing action of YHWH takes place in the historical processes of the political economy. Thus the indictment and the threat are real-time considerations: anti-neighborly uses of power produce destructive outcomes. The qualifying words of verse 13 do not change the defining calculus of this oracular truth-telling. YHWH will not long tolerate the reduction of neighbors to commodities.

Truth Moves against Power

In 11:14–40 we see the religious truth of Torah violation shaded over into political realism where power lives. We may imagine that a self-preoccupied power agent like Solomon was not much disturbed by religious talk. What more likely would impact such a concentration of power is counterpower of a worldly kind. In verses 14–22 and in verses 23–25, we have two political-military threats against Solomon that are introduced by the phrases, "The LORD raised up" and "God raised up" (vv. 14, 23). In both cases, the substance is a real threat with the muscle, respectively, of Egypt and of Syria.

But it is in verses 26–40 that we see the way in which, according to the narrative, truth moves against absolute power. Jeroboam, the lead figure in this account, was Solomon's Secretary of Forced Labor in the north (v. 28). He was well connected to the regime and knew about its exploitative practices from the inside. He is moved to action by the utterance of Ahijah, a prophet from the dissenting political priestly trajectory of Shiloh (v. 29). Thus the matter advances from the rhetoric of verses 9–12 in which there is no human agent, only YHWH. Now in verses 26–40, there is a political player matched to a prophetic utterer, that is, a truth-teller allied with a new political agent. Ahijah delivers an authorizing, summoning oracle that announces divine resolve (vv. 31–32) and that again concerns violation of Torah:

> This is because he has forsaken me, worshiped Astarte the goddess of the Sidonians, Chemosh the god of Moab, and Milcom the god of the Ammonites, and has not walked in

my ways, doing what is right in my sight and keeping my
statutes and my ordinances, as his father David did. (v. 33)

Jeroboam is offered power if he confirms Torah:

I will take you, and you shall reign over all that your soul
desires; you shall be king over Israel. If you will listen to
all that I command you, walk in my ways, and do what is
right in my sight by keeping my statutes and my commandments, as David my servant did. I will be with you, and will
build you an enduring house, as I built for David, and I will
give Israel to you. (vv. 37–38)

Jeroboam had to flee from Solomon who recognized him as
a threat (v. 40). But he will be back (12:2)!

The prophetic utterance is designed, in the text, to provide the backdrop and authorization for the revolutionary
political act that is to follow. This is an astonishing and
revolutionary utterance, for it uses the very rhetoric of the
divine promise to David for this militant anti-David.

The narrative of 12:1–19 reports on what was a hard-
nosed political struggle between the old power, with its
capacity to impose exploitative taxation, and the new, ris-
ing power of the recalcitrant north. The narrative is largely
political in its casting, except for the definitive comment of
verse 15:

So the king did not listen to the people, because it was a
turn of affairs brought about by the LORD that he might
fulfill his word, which the LORD had spoken by Ahijah the
Shilonite to Jeroboam son of Nebat.

The narrative clearly attests YHWH's hidden governance in the overthrow of Solomon's regime. It was YHWH
who caused Rehoboam, son of Solomon, to resist in foolish

ways the elders of the North! And Rehoboam, like every threatened tyrant, sends his most brutal agent to quell the revolt, in this case Adoniram, the enforcer of forced labor (v. 18; see 4:6). But it is too late for such absolutism! The king's agent was murdered and the king beat a hasty retreat to the safe citadel of Jerusalem. The north was lost, just as the truth-tellers had said.

Thus we can see the narrative development in chapters 11 and 12 that moves from theological assertion to political realism:

- 11:1–13 is covenantal theology without any human agent,
- 11:26–40 features a prophet who intrudes into political action, and
- 12:1–19 is preoccupied with political action with only a decisive trace of YHWH's engagement.

The failure of Solomonic power has theological roots. His power cannot be sustained in the face of Torah truth and prophetic implementation. But such truthfulness is not a religious fantasy; it receives public enactment through Solomon's subjects who refuse absolute power. The truth that challenges power is truth uttered by YHWH. But it is, at the same time, truth that arises as weary bodies find voice: "Your father made our yoke heavy. Now therefore lighten the hard service of your father and his heavy yoke that he placed on us, and we will serve you" (12:4).

The drama of the exodus is being reperformed in Israel! Absolute power is confronted by divine authorization and human bodily pain, a combination before which absolute power cannot be sustained.

THE TORAH OF TRUTH-TELLING

Thus the noble dream of chapter 3 ends in royal flight: "King Rehoboam then hurriedly mounted his chariot to flee to Jerusalem. So Israel has been in revolt against the house of David to this day" (12:18–19). No one could have imagined such an outcome for Solomon's regime, especially given the achievement of the temple. In chapter 8, the centerpiece of Solomon's many accomplishments, YHWH had been domesticated to dwell in the Holy of Holies as the patron, protector, and guarantor of the regime. That should have been enough. The temple gives visible religious expression to the capacity of Solomon for accumulation and commoditization.

But the truth sneaks in to such awesome claims for God-backed power. There is uneasiness even in the temple narrative, as though some around Solomon knew better and were not seduced by his absolutizing ideology. Some knew better; they recognized that Solomon's great achievement did not square with the freedom of the exodus God or with what was bearable economically and politically by the body politic over which Solomon presided. The uneasiness is voiced even in the temple narrative.

– In 8:9 it is observed amid the great festal procession of the ark of the covenant:

> There was nothing in the ark except the two tablets of stone that Moses had placed there at Horeb, where the LORD made a covenant with the Israelites, when they came out of the land of Egypt.

One might have expected witness to the awesome deity enthroned on the ark in splendor. But all there was were the two tablets with the Ten Commandments. That is all. We get the terse truth unadorned by liturgical enhancement. Right at the center of the temple liturgy, there are these uncompromising commandments.

- In 8:27 just in the midst of the glorious acclamation of divine presence in the temple, there is qualification about the presence of the God who hovers around Solomon's experiment:

"But will God indeed dwell on the earth? Even the heaven and the highest heaven cannot contain you, much less this house that I have built!"

This house of power cannot contain the God of truth! Because this is the God of transcendent freedom who will not be harnessed to any of our preferred power arrangements, no matter how wondrously appointed.[12]

- And finally, in what must be a derivative reflection, there is a meditation on exile:

"If they sin against you—for there is no one who does not sin—and you are angry with them and give them to an enemy, so that they are carried away captive to the land of the enemy far off or near; and if they come to their senses in the land to which they have been taken captive . . ." (8:46–47)

These verses are undoubtedly later than Solomon. But they are placed here by the tradition on Solomon's watch. They are placed here because this acutely discerning tradition knows and has always known, from Solomon onward, where this is all headed. They knew, not because they could predict. They knew because they did not doubt the truth of the Torah tradition with its demand and its sanctions.

The Torah of truth-telling knows that absolute power that defies covenantal reality will eventually lead to displacement!

READING AS CONTESTANTS

We are left in our contemporary mad scramble for commodity, to ponder the claim of this narrative that not even Solomon could find guarantees beyond his own greedy anxiety. With its surface celebration of Solomon, coupled with an ironic subversion of that celebration, the text permits Solomon to overwhelm the claims of truth. That royal overwhelming, however, is unsustainable.

Long after, as Jeremiah processed the destruction of Jerusalem that Solomon had set in motion, Jeremiah reduced the calculus of power and truth to a lean formula with two sets of triads:

> Do not let the wise boast in their wisdom, do not let the mighty boast in their might, do not let the wealthy boast in their wealth; but let those who boast in this, that they understand and know me, that I am the LORD; I act with steadfast love, justice, and righteousness in the earth, for in these things I delight, says the LORD. (Jer. 9:23–24)[13]

The initial triad in this oracle consists of *wisdom, might, and wealth*; these are most fully embodied, in ancient Israel, in Solomon who had so much about which to boast. That Solomonic triad, however, is countered by the prophet with the covenantal triad of *steadfast love, justice, and righteousness*. The poet sees that the deep contest of the human enterprise is summarized in these elemental terms. Solomon's awesome achievement is celebrated . . . and terminated.

In the wake of Jeremiah and the competing triads, Jesus tells a story about the fool who has his self-congratulations abruptly ended in death (Luke 12:16-21). The fool in the parable of course is not named. But he is surely the great accumulator in the imagination of Jesus. The story is followed by Jesus' didactic comment to his disciples (Luke 12:22–31). Jesus warns against anxiety about commodities: "Therefore I tell you, do not worry about your life, what you will eat, or about your body, what you will wear" (v. 22).

He identifies the restless, strong pursuit of commodities that make us secure, and contrasts that with other creatures who are free of such anxiety, folk like birds and flowers. And then he names the icon of commodity anxiety: "Yet I tell you, *even Solomon* in all his glory was not clothed like one of these" (v. 27).

It turns out that the fool in the parable is none other than Solomon, the quintessential accumulator propelled by profound anxiety. Jesus' testimony is that another way is possible, grounded in the goodness of God: "For it is the nations of the world that strive after all these things, and your Father knows that you need them" (v. 30).

The contest that Jeremiah summarizes and that Jesus sets before his followers is as old as Solomon. The tradition has always known about the deathliness of anxious power and about the life-giving truth of the covenant. The Solomonic narrative is, in the Old Testament, a compelling engagement of our interface of power and truth, an engagement as immediate as our anxious life in a world of endless accumulation.

NOTES

1. See Walter Brueggemann, *Solomon: Israel's Ironic Icon of Human Achievement* (Columbia: University of South Carolina Press, 2005), 238–42. For this discussion of Solomon more

generally, this book provides the background for my current interpretive comments.

2. William T. Cavanaugh, *The Myth of Religious Violence: Secular Ideology and the Roots of Modern Conflict* (Oxford: Oxford University Press, 2009); and *Migrations of the Holy: God, State, and the Political Meaning of the Church* (Grand Rapids: Eerdmans, 2011) has made a compelling case to show that religious institutions, in the end, are no more violent than are state institutions. Thus Solomon's attempt to overcome what was sectarian in ancient Israel was no guarantee that his state would be any less violent.

3. I have not attempted to sort out questions of historicity with reference to the traditions of Solomon, but I have tried to read the text as it is given to us. On such matters, see William G. Dever, *What Did the Biblical Writers Know and When Did They Know It?* (Grand Rapids: Eerdmans, 2001), 97–157.

4. Carolyn J. Sharp, *Irony and Meaning in the Hebrew Bible* (Bloomington: Indiana University Press, 2009), 49.

5. Wayne C. Booth, *The Rhetoric of Fiction,* 2nd ed. (Chicago: University of Chicago Press, 1983), 300.

6. See Sharp, *Irony and Meaning,* 220–38. Gail R. O'Day, *Revelation in the Fourth Gospel: Narrative Mode and Theological Claim* (Philadelphia: Fortress Press, 1986), 23, defines irony in this way: "saying one thing and meaning something else or saying something while pretending not to say it. . . . There is always some kind of opposition between the two levels of meaning in irony—either contradiction, incongruity, or incompatibility."

7. See an earlier narrative report on the same practice of seizing the concubines of the old king in 2 Samuel 16:20–23.

8. Reinhold Niebuhr, *The Irony of American History* (New York: Charles Scribner's, 1952).

9. See Genesis 41:1–7, 17–32 for Pharaoh's nightmare of scarcity.

10. Among the better expositions of David on this count, see Baruch Halpern, *David's Secret Demons: Messiah, Murderer, Traitor, King* (Grand Rapids: Eerdmans, 2001).

11. The listing of supervisors is not very different from the supervisors who assured Pharaoh's work in Exodus 5:14, though the terms used are not the same.

12. See 2 Samuel 17:14 for an earlier narrative account of the hidden governance of history by YHWH, and see the discussion of Gerhard von Rad, *The Problem of the Hexateuch and Other Essays* (New York: McGraw-Hill, 1966), 196–204.

13. On these verses, see Walter Brueggemann, *Journey to the Common Good* (Louisville, KY: Westminster John Knox Press, 2010), 56–72.

Chapter 3

TRUTH HAS ITS DAY

Elisha

THE BOOKS OF 1 AND 2 KINGS OFFER THE NORMATIVE HISTORY of the monarchal period of ancient Israel and ancient Judah. And even though it is commonly recognized that this material consists in theologically interpreted history, for the most part the sequence and time line of the work continues to guide critical interpretation. The historical sequence, traced over four hundred years, begins with the death of King David and the establishment of the surpassing power of his son, Solomon, a process I have traced in my last chapter (1 Kgs. 1–11). The sequence ends in 1 Kings 24–25 with the destruction of Jerusalem and its temple and the deportation of the leading citizens, including the royal family (2 Kgs. 24:13–17; 25:11-12), with an intriguing footnote added at the end (2 Kgs. 25:27–30).[1]

FORMULATING ROYAL HISTORY

Between the rise of Solomon and the destruction of Jerusalem the material traces the dynastic continuity of the family of David in Jerusalem and the several dynastic discontinuities in the northern kingdom of Israel in Samaria. This material, for the most part, is cast in a flat, formulaic style that is interrupted here and there by narrative where the theological interpreters want to make a point. Thus royal history is reduced mostly to formula, with a clever scheme whereby the royal histories of North and South are told in tandem. The formulaic quality of the account assures some symmetry and coherence to the whole and permits the theological interpreters to articulate the ways in which divine purpose, divine judgment, and divine fidelity impinge decisively on the historical process. The whole of the formulaic scheme seems to have a pedagogical intent, to make the sweep of the whole, with appropriate specificity, manageable.[2] The sum of the material is not unlike an account of fourth graders in U.S. public schools who memorize the names of all the U.S. presidents and the wars they fought and characteristically won.

There is no doubt that this sequence of royal rulers identifies the visible, recognized, and legitimate power players in Israelite history. These are the ones who have occupied office, made decisions, managed the economy, waged the wars, and built the temple, all the ingredients of public, visible power. And at least in the South of Jerusalem, it is understood to be power legitimated by YHWH's promise to the house of David and YHWH's residence in the Jerusalem temple (see 2 Sam. 7:11-16; 1 Kgs. 8:12-13). Like a fourth grader, the report is not intended that the reader should treat the claims of the material in a suspicious way or with any resistance. This is the given power arrangement of the acknowledged past of the community, an acknowledged past that connects the interpretive generation of the exile with the reassuring divine guarantees to the house of David.

ELIJAH ENTERS THE STORY

Except a strange thing happens in the midst of this tedious formulaic royal recital. That royal symmetry is abruptly interrupted in 1 Kings 17:1 by a completely unexpected departure from the royal categories. Without explanation or anticipation, we get this: "Now Elijah the Tishbite . . . said to Ahab." We are not ready for this as readers; and obviously King Ahab was not ready either. We have never heard of this fellow. We do not know anything about Tishbe, his place of origin. We do not know how he gained access to the king. We do not know how it was that he knew about the drought to come of which he spoke, nor about how he received—or claimed to have received—a word from YHWH that was to be relayed to the king. Everything remains unexplained! The historians give no effort to explanation. It is as though his appearance and utterance evoke no curiosity on their part, as though it all seems credible to them. Or perhaps they intend that the reader should be shocked and scandalized that royal history can be so strangely interrupted.

What we get of the towering figure of Elijah consists in four chapters of narrative, stories that are regularly framed by "Thus says the LORD," as though this uncredentialed, non-legitimated outsider could carry words of revelatory force that would challenge the settled power of the king, even as it challenged the settled formulations of the historical narrative. Nothing is ever explained about Elijah the Tishbite. He stays on his rampage of transformative action, confronting and challenging the power of the throne and creating, beyond royal control, zones of new life that defy any normal explanation. In 1 Kings 19:19–21, he summons and invests a disciple, Elisha, who is to follow him, follow in obedience and follow in succession:

> "Let me kiss my father and my mother, and then I will follow you." . . . Then he set out and followed Elijah, and became his servant. (vv. 20–21)

And then, in 2 Kings 2:9-12, Elijah is inexplicably and dramatically taken up into heaven before the very eyes of his disciples:

> "If you see me as I am being taken from you, it will be granted you; if not, it will not." As they continued walking and talking, a chariot of fire and horses of fire separated the two of them, and Elijah ascended in a whirlwind into heaven. (vv. 10–11)

Elijah leaves, even as he first appeared, abruptly and without explanation, in defiance of any normal rationality. As a result of this inscrutable "ascent into heaven," he did not die. His life does not receive any normal closure. Indeed, his life remains open to future possibility, as Malachi expected his return (Mal. 4:5–6), as some took Jesus of Nazareth to be Elijah returned (Matt. 16:24), as some thought Jesus on the cross was summoning him (Matt. 27:49), and even as Jews in our own time expect Elisha to reappear at the Passover table. How unnerving in royal history, with its buttoned-down formulations of power, to have this inexplicable, inscrutable agent loosed in the historical process, subject to none of the conventional forms of power and explained by none of the conventional modes of reason! How unnerving to have such a character occupy the middle chapters of the royal history, displacing the formulas of control and certitude, so that the reader must watch, wide-eyed, to see what the next violation of royal power might be. This Elijah has no tools of authority beyond the awesome formula, "Thus says the LORD," whereby he claimed to be—and was seen to be—a truth-carrier; they noticed, as they remembered and imagined him, that his *utterance of truth* in the name of YHWH was matched by his *performance of truth* in the lives of the vulnerable. The narratives about him have continuing subversive force because they can never be accommodated to the more convenient categories of royal administration.

ELISHA CONTINUES ELIJAH'S WORK

This Elijah, once he has disappeared into heaven (from whence he may "come again") is followed by his disciple Elisha.[3] Elisha watched the ascent of Elijah into heaven and cried out to him in berement (2 Kgs. 2:12). And then, abruptly, he takes up his mantle of empowerment that he had received from Elijah (2:14; see 1 Kgs. 19:19) and is seen to possess (or be possessed by the "spirit of Elijah" [2 Kgs. 2:15]); he immediately begins his own career of astonishing transformative power. Elisha continues and extends the force of Elijah's work and, in a more extended narrative, continues as an unnerving, inexplicable presence in the midst of royal history. While the kings continue to occupy and control the totems of power, it is clear in this telling that the "holy has migrated" from royal office to these uncredentialed agents who are given ample narrative time in the telling of royal history.[4]

The two of them together, Elijah and Elisha, occupy the narrative from 1 Kings 17 through 2 Kings 9, and since the books of Kings altogether consist in forty-seven chapters, we can see that these two characters occupy one-fourth of the whole of the history of royal Israel and royal Judah. Imagine—they account for 25 percent of the whole, for they have clearly captured and occupied the imagination of these theological historians who dare to tell their history by putting them at the center of the narrative. It makes one wonder how they got that material past the royal censors!

This remarkable narrative achievement suggests that these theological historians suspect—and mean to communicate—that the occupants of royal power are not the definitive players in the true history of this people; the real players are Elijah and Elisha who stand outside and beyond the routines of power, acting variously in defiance or disregard of these occupants of the seats and forms of power.

Such a rendering of public history would be like telling the long history of South Africa and devoting primary attention to Nelson Mandela and Desmond Tutu as the real makers of history. Or perhaps it would be like featuring Martin Luther King Jr. and Daniel Berrigan and Susan B. Antoinette as the key players in U.S. history, or Dietrich Bonhoeffer as the key player in German history, or Thomas Cranmer as the key player in English history, or John Calvin as the key player in European history, or Oscar Romero and Pope John XXIII and Hans Kung as the key players in the long history of the church. The key players, it turns out, are those who refuse to be credentialed or curbed by traditional modes of power, who understand that the transformative power of truth is not a credible companion for consolidating modes of established power, but that truth characteristically runs beyond the confines of such power. Clearly those who wrote and edited the books of Kings had a playful, emancipatory sense of history and were not overly impressed with dynastic categories, because real power is the capacity to speak the truth and to enact transformative, truthful ways at the behest of the spirit who is not contained in royal horizon. The daring energy to narrate this alternative history functions, inevitably, to expose the kings who are entrusted with power as being fundamentally without power to transform.[5] The outcome is to delegitimize and deconstruct the kings in effective ways in order to show that while they occupy the forms of power, they lack the substance of power. They are not entrusted with the truth that makes power effective. In the end, it seems plausible that 1 and 2 Kings might in fact be titled, "1 and 2 Kings?" with a lingering question mark and a wink to indicate that the royal recital is not to be taken with too much seriousness. The kings turn out to be, in this telling, simply window dressing for the carriers of truth who exhibit and enact transformative power that is kept for us in narrative modes. Thus the narratives of Elisha place an accent on *truth* that simply disregards *power.* Elisha does not challenge the kings but proceeds in his transformative ways in total disregard of royal posturing.

The same subversion of power by truth is evident in the way in which Luke begins his account of Jesus of Nazareth. Luke is at pains to put his readers on notice that this is no ordinary history. He has an angel anticipate cousin John by saying, "with the spirit and power of Elijah he will go before him" (1:17). He has Gabriel declare that "nothing will be

impossible with God" (1:37). He offers us an alternative genealogy that refuses the royal recital of Matthew and provides
a list of the uncredentialed, rather like *Roots* by Alex Haley
that traces a genealogy that the plantation masters never sus-
pected (Luke 3:23–38).[6] In the midst of this playful subversion, Luke has John go public in the empire. He does so by
locating the reader amid all the recognized totems of power:

> In the fifteenth year of the reign of emperor Tiberius, when
> Pontius Pilate was governor of Judea, and Herod was ruler
> of Galilee, and his brother Philip ruler of the region of
> Ituraea and Trachonitis, and Lysanias ruler of Abilene,
> during the high-priesthood of Annas and Caiaphas, . . .
> (Luke 3:1-2a)

And then, abruptly:

> The word of God came to John son of Zechariah in the
> wilderness. He went into all the region around the Jordan,
> proclaiming a baptism of repentance for the forgiveness of
> sins. (vv. 2b–3)

In this skillful rhetoric, Luke dismisses as irrelevant all the
aforementioned power players. They are irrelevant because
the new center of human history comes in a power surge
that the established powers could neither co-opt nor resist:

> Jesus, *full of the Holy Spirit*, returned from the Jordan and
> was led by the Spirit in the wilderness. (Luke 4:1)

> Then Jesus, *filled with the power of the Spirit*, returned to
> Galilee. (4:14)

> "The Spirit of the Lord is upon me." (4:18)

The last is a quote, of course, but the point is the same. The
new history of the world is powered by the Spirit that leaves
us free from the categories of established, visible power.

The Elijah-Elisha narrative is a precursor and model for the story of Jesus that Luke has to tell. This strand of biblical imagination, in both Testaments, distrusts the managers of official power and dismisses them from center stage. This counter-imagination names and proposes an alternative account of the history of this people and of the world.

How odd! And how cunning! The narrative does not perform this dismissal directly and does not offer this alternative frontally. That would be too dangerous . . . and too easy. It does so in the subversive mode of narrative testimony, so that the subversive mode of telling matches the subversive substance. It summons the reader to step outside conventional rationality in order to recognize the point of the testimony. It does so by observing for us that the real action of transformation is *elsewhere*, not where we have been socialized to look for it.

Thus I pondered, as I anticipated this Episcopalian conversation, that the Episcopal Church, even as an establishment operation like its companion churches, meets regularly in its liturgy to deconstruct and dismiss the managers of power and to show and attest that the real action, guided by God's spirit of truth, is somewhere else, sometimes in the body of Christ and broadly in the sweep of God's own spirit in the affairs of the world. That liturgy, like these ancient narratives, is inherently subversive; even though we do all that we can to make it come out conventionally as business as usual. The reason we cannot finally have the narrative and the testimony and the liturgy in a safe way is precisely because its subversive texture is intrinsic to the material itself, not imposed by any particular interpretation. In what follows, I consider the ways in which the narrative attests that the real action—the dangerous, transformative

action—swirls around these truth-carriers who are uncredentialed, without power, without pedigree, but who are
infused with a dangerous spirit of transformation, alive in
the world, transforming the world to well-being. The managers of conventional power stand at the edge of the narrative, bewildered but helpless to impede or assist this force
in the world. This transformative capacity, anciently visible
in these stories and contemporarily available in these narratives, is seen to be deeply in sync with the mystery of the
God who wills a just, peaceable world.

THE NATURE OF POWER AND THE CLAIM
OF TRUTH

In what follows I invite you to read again these stories, some
of which are familiar to us. But now I hope that you will
read them as a sustained contest about the nature of power
and the claim of truth. This contestation concerns the reliability and effectiveness of established concentrations of
power vis-à-vis the uncredentialed, transformative power
that is visible from time to time in the public processes of
history. This contestation is a serious and sustained one;
here it is conducted through narrative specificity. Unless we
are shrewdly discerning about the thick contestation that is
enacted here, we are likely to mistake these narratives for no
more than incidental legendary episodes, a mistake that has
pervaded much critical scholarship.

The name *Elisha* means, "my God saves." The one who
is "my God" is none other than YHWH, the God of exodus transformation, a name that is sounded in the earlier
Elijah, which means "YHWH is my God," for the "jah" in
his name refers to YHWH. The claim of both names, Elijah

and Elisha, is that no one else, no other God, can save. No other power can heal or feed or restore or transform. In local setting, the two names constitute a defiance and dismissal of Baal who cannot save (see 1 Kgs. 18:21, 39). But of course the contestation runs well beyond any local Baal to every competitor to YHWH. The actions of these characters give substance to the claim that "my God saves," for "my God" enacts rescue through these empowered human agents to whom the text bears witness.

Already in 2 Kings 2, when Elisha received the mantel of Elijah and the spirit of Elijah, the first thing he does is to head east across the Jordan. We are told that he "struck the water, saying, 'Where is the LORD, the God of Elijah?' When he had struck the water, the water was parted to the one side and to the other, and Elisha went over" (v. 14). He parted the Jordan! He went over on dry ground. But of course every reader and every witness knows that the parting of the Jordan is a replica and a reiteration of the parting of the waters of the Red Sea. Thus it is remembered: "For the LORD your God dried up the waters of the Jordan for you until you crossed over, as the LORD your God did to the Red Sea, which he dried up for us until we crossed over" (Josh. 4:23).

The as connects the remembered exodus and the enacted crossing.[7] This is the new Moses! This is the new emancipator who will bring life to this people. Elisha is now cast as the one who will defy the power of enslavement and death for the sake of life. He will do so as Moses did, recognizing, as did Moses, that the power of death has taken up residence among the socio-economic, political powers that monopolize life to the exclusion of many. That exclusive control of life is managed by the regime of Ahab and his sons who become the counterpoint to Elisha in these narratives.

ELISHA ENACTS LIFE

In 2 Kings 4, we are given three narratives concerning the way in which Elisha, the uncredentialed carrier of God's truth, enacts life in completely inexplicable ways.

Abundance for the Needy

Elisha is addressed by a widow in his circle of companions (vv. 1–7). She "cries out" in shrill protest against systemic abuse because her creditor is about to seize her children as slaves for payment of her debt that she cannot pay. Elisha wades into an acute economic crisis that features the haves devouring the have-nots and their children. He counters that situation of hopelessness by an inscrutable act of abundance (vv. 2–6). We are not told how he produces such an overflow of olive oil. It is more than enough to overwhelm the entire village. Elisha refuses to participate in the scarcity system that is created and exploited by the creditor in a way that victimizes the widow. He breaks the social disease of scarcity by an awesome act of abundance.

The outcome is that the widow can pay her debts, rescue her children, and live safely on the residue of the abundance of olive oil. We may pause over the fact that the miracle performed by Elisha in verses 2–6 is sandwiched in the narrative by an *economic crisis* (v. 1) and an *economic restoration* (v. 7). It is impossible to assess or appreciate the force or significance of the miracle unless we attend to its economic framing. The dominant economic frame of credit and debt is created and certified by conventional power, by government in collusion with banking institutions. But Elisha tells and acts the truth that confounds such power. The truth he enacts is that there is an abundance of life resources, and they are freely given to the "undeserving" widow and her friend in the village. The narrative remaps the social grid of power according to the truth of God-given abundance.

Life Reverses Death

The extended narrative of verses 8–37 tells the complicated tale of the way in which Elisha gives a son to a woman who has no son (vv. 11–17), how the son died (vv. 18–31), and how Elisha decisively intervened in the life of the woman who faced the death of her son (vv. 32–37). Elisha has no hesitation about moving into the zone of death. He prays over the dead boy (v. 33). He makes physical contact with the dead boy—mouth to mouth, eye to eye, hand to hand! The child sneezes and comes alive. Elisha says tersely to the astonished mother, "Take your son" (v. 36). The narrative is completely without curiosity or explanation. It does not tell us how the death of the boy is overcome. But it does not doubt the wonder enacted because it gladly attests that Elisha is infused with power to make all things new.

Food for the Hungry

After the purification of food (vv. 38–41), Elisha comes across hungry people (vv. 42–44). With a tiny bit of food for starters, he feeds them all. They are all fed! And there was a surplus left over, another sign that Elisha has the power of abundance entrusted to him, a power that overcomes deathly scarcity. By this time it does not surprise us that Elisha does such actions without narrative explanation. The absence of explanation is part of the narrative strategy so that the reader can see that, of course, that is what Elisha does; that is who he is in a way that does not require or even permit further comment. He is the master of new possibility, transforming situations of negativity into options for new life. We note that in all these narratives there is no other source of help, no king who can act, even though we are reading the book of *Kings*. That narrative absence of the kings exhibits and calls attention to the irrelevance of kings for the well-being of the realm that is rooted in a very different source.

ELISHA DRAWS A DIFFERENT POWER MAP

The power map of the narrative in 2 Kings 5 is somewhat different and more complex. Here the presenting problem—the human crisis—is leprosy that has struck a Syrian (Aramean) general; the general, Naaman, is afflicted with leprosy, a career-ending social disease. He finds his way to Samaria at the behest of an Israelite slave girl. He is directed by her to "the prophet" (v. 3). But like power-people characteristically, he misunderstands. He goes not to the prophet, but to the center of power, to see the Israelite king in Samaria (5:5–6). But the Israelite king dismisses his inquiry and his need: "Am I God, to give death or life, that this man sends word to me to cure a man of his leprosy?" (v. 7).

The king is outraged that this foreign general would come to him for help; he cannot help! He is not God, and healing requires God. The withdrawal of the king from the narrative exposes the king as an irrelevance. The one with all the power can do nothing to save. Because it is only "my God who saves."

Elisha, on the alert, invites the frustrated foreign general to come to him for help. Again the general, power-person that he is, misconstrues. He arrives at the door of the prophet with a great impressive retinue (v. 9). He expected to be greeted as an "important person"! But Elisha is not impressed with such a show of power. Characteristically he is not impressed with such power. He knows that the regalia of military power mean nothing. He will not even get up from his chair to see the visiting dignitary. He only leaves instruction to dip into the Jordan seven times. The instruction sounds like the familiar, "Take two aspirins." The Syrian general is indignant. He does not think he has been taken seriously or with due regard. He thinks his affliction merits more careful attention than that, and he does not want to rely on a general public health plan. He wishes that he had never made this face-losing journey into enemy territory to get help (vv. 11–12).

But finally, after much coaxing and negotiation, the general obeys the prophet. He enters the Jordan River, even though he does so with loud protests. And then, says the narrative: "His flesh was restored like the flesh of a young boy, and he was clean" (v. 14).

He was cleansed of his social disease! He was saved! He can return to his prestigious role in Damascus. It is as the little slave girl had assured—the prophet can heal. Naaman wants to pay Elisha for the healing, as medical service is expensive, especially if you do not have coverage in a foreign country. But Elisha refuses. The general need not pay. But he does break out in doxology to the God who saves and heals: "'Now I know that there is no God in all the earth except in Israel'" (v. 15).

That part of the narrative ends with Elisha's capacity for healing confirmed and with YHWH's transformative power on exhibit. (And on the side, unmentioned and unnoticed, is the unnamed king in Samaria.) The narrative portrays the way in which this strutting royal power from the Syrian world must submit to the inscrutable capacity of this outsider. The power map of the world is changed; for a moment the general grasps the truth with which he is confronted. He will not stay in that awareness very long, for he admits to the prophet:

> "But may the LORD pardon your servant on one count: when my master goes into the house of Rimmon to worship there, leaning on my arm, and I bow down in the house of Rimmon, when I do bow down in the house of Rimmon, may the LORD pardon your servant on this one count." (v. 18)

He must go home and worship local gods. But Elisha does not care. He is not into "church growth." It is enough to have enacted a new life in the world of power. He has no rebuke for the general but says only, "'Go in peace'" (v. 19). Go in *shalom, shalom* given by God, enacted by this truth-laden outsider.

In 6:8–23, the king in Samaria appears again, only to be reduced yet again to an irrelevance. In the war with Syria the primary interaction in the narrative is between the Syrian king, who is obsessed with a security leak, and Elisha, who counters that anxious king with his inexplicable authority. Who would have imagined that this uncredentialed transformer would be a match, more than a match, for the king of Syria! The Syrian king, in his anxiety, seeks to arrest this troublesome man of God, because he is the source of the leaks in the war plans of Syria (vv. 11–14). But the prophet outflanks the king! He makes visible to his aide allies that are beyond the ken of the king. And then he prays the king blind (v. 18). As a consequence, the Syrian king becomes the captive of the prophet. Elisha has yet again trumped one agent of official power.

Only then, belatedly, the Israelite king enters the narrative (v. 21). He wants to do what kings always do, namely, kill the enemy (v. 21). Elisha, however, refuses such conventional lethal royal conduct. Indeed, he denies the king in Samaria any authority at all over the captured king of Syria. Even in his own capitol city, the king is powerless before the positive resolve of the prophet. Everything the prophet is able to do is premised on his odd truth that eludes the two kings: "'Do not be afraid, for there are more with us than there are with them'" (v. 16).

The prophet knew more about alliances (with chariots) and resources (invisible horses) than the king could ever discern or muster. And so, in his odd but unchallenged authority, Elisha commands his own king: "Set food and water before them so that they may eat and drink; and let them go to their master" (v. 22). The king prepares a feast; the enemy eats and goes home:

> So he prepared for them a great feast; after they ate and drank, he sent them on their way, and they went to their master. And the Arameans no longer came raiding into the land of Israel. (vv. 23–24)

Imagine a great feast! A great feast put before the enemy. A great feast embodies abundance. Perhaps the king has such an abundance available, but he operates out of a narrow scarcity. It took the magisterial mandate of this truthteller to summon this agent of power into new behavior. That new behavior of generous hospitality broke the pattern of violence. The king knew or understood nothing of this. He obeys only because what is now possible and what is now required is beyond the zone of his power. It is the transformative truthfulness of Elisha that allows and permits the king to act out of abundance of which he did not know he was capable.

A MIGHTY WIND

Finally of the Elisha narratives I will mention the complex story in 2 Kings 6:24–7:20 that again exhibits Elisha as the restorer of social health. Scarcity has caused such high prices for food that the widows cannot afford to buy any food. There is a famine in the land, an acute scarcity. It is so acute that two mothers dispute the eating of their own children. So desperate is one of these mothers that she cries out to the king, the one who is expected to step into the scarcity with some help: "'Help, my Lord king!'" (v. 26).

The king refutes her with a response that is not unlike that of the king in 5:7: "No! Let the LORD help you. How can I help you? From the threshing floor or from the wine press?" (v. 27). The king has no capacity to help. He cannot manufacture food. He cannot cause grain on the threshing floor or wine from the wine press. He has no store of abundance from which to respond. He is powerless before the famine and, as in chapter 5, the king appeals to God: Only God can heal a leper. Only God can respond to the famine. And the king is clearly not God!

But the king, in his acute anxiety and impotence, goes one better. He makes a royal threat against Elisha that is something of a non sequitur: "'So may God do to me, and more, if the head of Elisha son of Shaphat stays on his shoulders today'" (v. 31). At the same time he looks beyond Elisha to blame God: "'This trouble is from the LORD! Why should I hope in the LORD any longer?'" (v.33). The king, master of the power apparatus, ends in complete despair. He is an irrelevance, and he knows he is an irrelevance. He also knows that somewhere in the mix of God and Elisha there is a positive alternative. But he cannot engage that reality because the risk to his own power is too great.

That is the last time that the king will speak in this story. Now it is Elisha who occupies center stage. He promises, without telling us how, that by "tomorrow" there will be enough food so that the prices will go down and even the poor can buy food and eat (7:1). He knows that famines always cost the poor. Along the way, he condemns and dismisses the royal officer who supports the king, assuring him that he would get none of the food when it is again available (v. 2).

Then there is a strange narrative pause, as though we have a story within the story (vv. 3–8). We watch while the frightened Syrians abandon their military encampment because of their fear. When they flee in fear, they leave behind great stores of food. The cause of their fear, we are told, was a great wind that caused them to flee. They mistook the wind for the threat of a coming enemy. They fled before the wind. The narrative knows that this is no accidental or ordinary wind:

> For the Lord had caused the Aramean army to hear the sound of chariots and of horses, the sound of a great army, so that they said to one another, "The King of Israel has hired the kings of the Hittites and the king of Egypt to fight against us." (v. 6)

This NRSV rendering is too weak, because the Hebrew has three-fold "sound" (*qol*):

The *sound* of chariots,
The *sound* of horses,
The *sound* of a great army.

It was only a wind. But the wind sounded to them, in their fear, like a military threat. It was God who gave the wind. It was God who has acted surreptitiously to fulfill the word of Elisha that an abundance of food would cause lower prices and effectively end the starvation.

The food brought new possibility to the hungry crowd. The wind sent by YHWH has done what the king was unable to do! Elisha had promised at the outset:

"Tomorrow about this time a measure of choice meal shall be sold for a shekel, and two measures of barley for a shekel, at the gate of Samaria." (v. 1; see verse 18)

And then it is reported:

So a measure of choice meal was sold for a shekel, and two measures of barley for a shekel, according to the word of the LORD. (v. 16)

Between the anticipation of Elisha and the vindication of Elisha, there is a mighty wind. The crowd surged, so much so that it trampled the royal officer who was supervising the food distribution (v. 17). The captain did indeed not get any food, as the prophet had anticipated. Thus the famine was over, the crowd has abundance, and the royal apparatus has been routed and exposed as dysfunctional. Most important of all, the word of Elisha has prevailed. Only "my God can save."

THE POWER OF YHWH
AND THE IRRELEVANCE OF THE KING

The sum of these several narratives is massive in its claim. There has been a series of inexplicable transformations:

- poverty is turned to abundance
- death is turned to life
- hunger is turned to food
- war is turned to peace
- famine is turned to cheap food for the crowd

All of this is accomplished, so attests the narratives, by the inexplicable power and authority of Elisha. He

- caused the overflow of olive oil for the desperate widow,
- restored the son to life,
- fed the hungry assemblage and left a surplus of food,
- served a feast to the Syrians,
- healed the foreign leper, and
- overcame the famine.

Elisha broke the vicious cycles of deathliness before which all parties had become helpless.

And the king is at best irrelevant:

- the king is absent in the narratives of chapter 4
- in chapter 5, the king declares that he cannot heal leprosy, because he is not God (5:7)
- in chapter 6, the king only wants to kill his enemies, the Syrians, not feed them
- in chapter 7, the king declares that he is helpless in the face of the famine

These are the cadences of these narratives:

- they offer a series of wondrous transformations
- the transformations are wrought by Elisha, "my God saves"
- Elisha acts in place of the king who can do no mighty work

The narratives, taken in their cumulative impact, tell the true story of public life in Israel. The official managers of power are an irrelevance when they are not an impediment to the evocation of *shalom*. New possibility comes from Elisha who knows the truth of YHWH's rule and who does not compromise that rule for the sake of conventional power. Real power lies elsewhere, outside the regime . . . so the stories attest.

Thus we have a narratively constructed world that features *inexplicable transformations* wrought by *an uncredentialed character* who bears the truth concerning God's power in the world to the *exclusion of the king*. Even though this king occupies the forms of power, he is irrelevant to crisis situations—even on his own watch—that cry out for transformative intervention. Help comes, characteristically, from this unexpected, unexplained agent; help comes not at all from the source to whom we might expect to look.

It occurs to me that this casting of narrative after narrative gives specificity to the doxological claims of Psalm 146. The Psalm contrasts the ones who are no help with the true source of real help:

> Do not put our trust in princes,
>   in mortals, in whom there is *no help*.
> When their breath departs, they return to the earth;
>   on that very day their plans perish.

Happy are those whose *help is the God of Jacob,*
whose hope is in the L ORD their God.
(vv. 3–5)

The princes lack *ruah*: their breath departs. They are
helpless and impotent. By contrast, YHWH is the source
of help and the ground of hope. And then the Psalm supplies a doxological inventory of YHWH's transformative
capabilities:

who made heaven and earth,
the sea, and all that is in them;
who keeps faith forever;
who exercutes justice for the oppressed;
who gives food to the hungry.

The L ORD sets the prisoner freed;
the L ORD opens the eyes of the blind.
The L ORD lifts up those who are bowed down;
the L ORD loves the righteous.
The L ORD watches over the strangers;
he upholds the orphan and the widow,
but the way of the wicked he brings to ruin.
(vv. 6–9)

The Psalm credits such actions for the oppressed, the
hungry, the prisoner, the bowed down, the widow, and the
orphan to YHWH. But our narrative corpus details the way
in which the transformative power of YHWH is performed
through human agency to effect such change in the world.
And if princes, like the ones in our narratives, lack *ruah*,
we know from the outset of the Elisha narrative that Elisha
has a double portion of the same *ruah* that powered Elijah. It is clear that our narrative corpus, like the doxological
Psalm, attests that where YHWH's help, YHWH's hope,
and YHWH's spirit are deployed, the world is made new.

This human truth-carrier is the one who renews the world. Elisha does so, precisely on behalf of YHWH who "keeps faith forever" (v. 6). The word that is translated "faith" in NRSV in verse 6 is *'emeth*, a term that has the connotation of "true" or "reliable." The truthful reliability of YHWH, enacted through Elisha, is in stark contrast to the vacuous power of the kings, the one dismissed in the psalm and the ones disregarded in the narrative.

READING THE ELISHA NARRATIVES

We are left with wonderment about how to read the Elisha narratives: We may read them, as *critical scholars* tend to do: as legends. That is, as folk tales that are not historically reliable and that need not be taken seriously.[8] At best they have been treasured by naive people who innocently believed what could not be verified in any reasonable way. Such a dismissive reading trusts the claims of the royal record over such legends. But such a critical judgment, even if quite common, simply reflects the fact that critical scholarship, from the outset, has trusted the reason of modernity that looks askance at such narrative renderings of reality that, for the most part, must be explained away or at least treated with dismissive suspicion.

If, however, we are more inclined to trust the testimony of the text, we may see these narratives as accents of the surge of God's Spirit, as that holy wind blows where it will without respect for established forms of reason. Such *a fide-istic perspective* might link such stories to the later Christian traditions of Pentecost, so that the narratives are seen to attest the boundary-crossing, authority-defying freedom of God. Such a rendering easily connects these stories to the parallel stories of Jesus and eventually to the story of the church in the book of Acts wherein the imperial authorities of Rome regularly summon the church to account, but the church will not be stopped in its work of "'turning the world upside down'" (Acts 17:6). Such a reading sees that in real, concrete life, the power of God is indeed for "salvation" (Rom. 1:16).

One can, from that Pentecostal perspective, also approach these narratives with socio-economic, political realism to recognize that they constitute nothing less than *a counter-history*, an alternative reading of historical reality among those who are not enthralled by either the reason of established power or the totalizing symbols and icons that bespeak authority. Those who remain outside the totalizing claims of such establishment power are not only suspicious of and resistant to such claims. They may also be alert to the juices of transformation that authorize and evoke revolutionary courage that is concerned with the bodily transformation of those whose bodies have been effectively excluded from the body politic. On this reading, these narratives attest that God's reliable truthfulness has been unleashed in the world via human agency. As a consequence, we who hear and treasure and retell and reinterpret these stories are not to linger too long over status quo management categories. Because if we linger too long there and credit such categories too much, then we will be paralyzed and immobilized about new possibilities. We will be left cynical about and resistant to the claims of these narratives.

Our reading of truth that proceeds in disregard of power reaches readily into the New Testament. We may best turn to the Gospel of Luke, the great narrative of the Spirit. In his inaugural, Jesus comes to Nazareth (4:14-30). The narrative report begins with reference to the Spirit:

> Then Jesus, filled with the power of the Spirit, returned to Galilee, and a report about him spread through all the surrounding country. He began to teach in their synagogues and was praised by everyone. (vv. 14–15)

In the synagogue in Nazareth, he read from Isaiah 61, again with reference to the spirit:

> "The spirit of the Lord is upon me,
>   because he has anointed me to bring good news to
>   the poor.
> He has sent me to proclaim release to the captives
>   and recovery of sight to the blind,
>   to let the oppressed go free,
> to proclaim the year of the Lord's favor.
> (vv. 18–19)

And when he must dispute with the people in the synagogue, he will first mention how Elijah ended the drought in 1 Kings and ministered to a foreign widow:

> Truly I tell you, no prophet is accepted in the prophet's hometown. But the truth is, there were many widows in Israel in the time of Elijah, when the heaven was shut up three years and six months, and there was a severe famine over all the land; yet Elijah was sent to none of them except to a widow at Zarephath in Sidon. (vv. 24–26)

And then, in verse 27, he draws the argument toward Elisha and the narrative in 2 Kings 5 that we have referenced:

> "There were also many lepers in Israel in the time of the prophet Elisha, and none of them was cleansed except Naaman the Syrian."

The references to Elijah and Elisha constitute a way of identifying Jesus' own purpose as one outside the domain of established power; for good reason his statement evoked deep hostility from those who advocate and benefit from such established power:

> When they heard this, all in the synagogue were filled with rage. They got up, drove him out of town, and led him to the brow of the hill on which their town was built, so that they might hurl him off the cliff. (vv. 28–29)

It is no accident, of course, that in the dispute Jesus will appeal to these uncredentialed truth-carriers as a way to illumine his own uncredentialed truth-carrying vocation.

This witness to subversive reality extends in the Gospel of Luke from the Song of Mary through his answer to John and eventually to the testimony of Peter before the high priest:

> He has shown strength with his arm;
>   he has scattered the proud in the thought of their hearts.
> He has brought down the powerful from their thrones,
>   and lifted up the lowly;
> he has filled the hungry with good things,
>   and sent the rich away empty.
>
> (1:51–53)

> "Go and tell John what you have seen and heard: the blind receive their sight, the lame walk, the lepers are cleansed, the deaf hear, the dead are raised, the poor have good news brought to them. And blessed is anyone who takes no offense at me." (7:22–23)

> "We must obey God rather than any human authority." (Acts 5:29)

It is all part of one piece! The surge of the Spirit generates social upheavals that entrenched power cannot negate and social possibility that entrenched power cannot halt. Thus the case builds for the tense interface of power and truth.

Comparing the Old and New Testaments

We might now reflect on the moves I have made thus far toward the New Testament:

- Concerning Moses' interface with Pharaoh, I have quoted Mark 6:52: "They did not understand about the loaves, but their hearts were hardened."
- In the case of Solomon's absolutism, I have quoted Luke 12:27: "Yet I tell you, even Solomon in all his glory was not clothed like one of these."
- And now with reference to Elisha, I have quoted Luke 4:27: "There were also many lepers in Israel in the time of the prophet Elisha, and none of them was cleansed except Naaman the Syrian."

In these several performances Jesus is shown to be the way, the truth, and the life. He is presented as juxtaposed to established power in the same way as was Moses in his confrontation with Pharaoh, as were the adversaries of Solomon in their irony, and as was the outrageous freedom of Elisha who outruns his would-be royal opponents.

And now, among us, belatedly, the church has put trust in that same enactment of truthfulness that refuses power. It is now more common to hear stories like the following.

- Here is a pediatrician who arranges unused medical supplies as a resource for the poor who have no health coverage.
- Here is a college chaplain who one night stops to talk with prostitutes on the street in their despair. She initiates a program of dignity and protection that spreads

to other cities in a way that breaks the deathly drama of power and powerlessness.

- Here is an old-line denomination that at last, at long last, opens its doors to some too-long excluded.
- Here is a high school kid who goes to enough work camps to grow up to be a critical scholar who advocates for equality in a world of abusive inequality.

The story of Elisha is indeed news about life resources being found and performed where we did not expect to find them. The news enacted by Elisha is reperformed by Jesus. It is, subsequently, performed in many other venues, sometimes by the followers of Jesus, sometimes by others who stand alongside the faithful followers of Jesus. In every such performance of the news, it is Gospel truth enacted as practical transformation that settled power can neither enact nor prevent.

THE STORY OF ELISHA:
READING AS CONTESTANTS

I finish with two Elisha texts that will never make the lectionary; two texts that serve to frame the entire Elisha corpus. At the very beginning of his narrative Elisha must already have evoked great hostility, because he enacted truthfulness in a way that exposed the untruth of conventional power. Given that evocation of hostility, we are told, some small boys came out in the street to mock him. They were perhaps acting out the hostility to which their parents had given voice. They cried out against the prophet, "'Go away, baldhead! Go away, baldhead!'" (2 Kgs. 2:23). They made

fun of him and wanted to discredit him. But Elisha is no
pushover. It is reported that he responded to them harshly.
And when he did, two she-bears came out of the woods and
mauled forty-two boys. That is what it says! That is all it
says! Nobody speculates on where the she-bears came from
or who sent them. And God is not mentioned in this little
story. The bears come as an enactment of Elisha's curse
of the boys. But clearly Elisha has powers on his side that
are inescapable. The force, it would seem, is with him! The
claim is that Elisha is protected. The suggestion is that all
those who follow him in his transformative vocation will be
kept safe. Perhaps the phrase is, "Take heart!" Be fearless in
the face of impotent power. God has counted the hairs on
your head (Matt. 10:29–31). More than that, God has taken
sides with the bald guy and with many others who walk
the walk. Nothing can stop the walk, the march, of God's
transformative truth that is marching on. Elisha is perhaps a
precursor of those who later on will sing, "We are marching
in the light of God."[9]

That text at the beginning of the Elisha narrative is
matched by an equally curious text at the end (2 Kgs. 13:20–
21). After Elisha has died and been buried, they tried hurriedly to hide another dead body on top of his body in the
grave. They placed the dead body on top of Elisha's dead
body. And when they did so, we are told: "As soon as the
man touched the bones of Elisha, he came to life and stood
on his feet" (v. 21).

It turns out that Elisha, in death as in life, is radioactive.
His body is seen to be life-giving, even in death. Thus his
very existence assures that the world would stay open to
possibility. Contact with him is life-giving! The drama runs
from *the two she-bears* in chapter 2 to the *radioactive corpse* in

chapter 13. And between the two the narrative teems with wonders that outrun explanation. Established power specializes in explanations. But Gospel truth does not wait for that. It rushes on to new life.

NOTES

1. I have anticipated some of this argument in *Testimony to Otherwise: The Witness of Elijah and Elisha* (St. Louis: Chalice Press, 2001), but I now see with much greater clarity the fundamental contestation that is conducted in these narratives.

2. It is possible to think that the whole of the narrative of Kings is designed as a theodicy to justify YHWH's destruction of Jerusalem; such an argument would function for Judah in the way that 2 Kings 17:7–23 functions as a theodicy concerning the fall of northern Israel.

3. See Walter Brueggemann, "Elisha as the Original Pentecost Guy," *Journal of Preachers* 32, no. 4 (Pentecost, 2009): 41–47.

4. I take the phrase "migration of the holy" from William T. Cavanaugh, *The Myth of Religious Violence: Secular Ideology and the Root of Modern Conflict* (Oxford: Oxford University Press, 2009), 174 and *passim;* and *Migrations of the Holy: God, State, and the Political Meaning of the Church* (Grand Rapids: Eerdmans, 2011). Cavanaugh, in turn, has appropriated the phrase from the work of John Bossy.

5. For a contemporary counter-history, see Howard Zinn, *A People's History of the United States* (San Francisco: Harper & Row, 1980).

6. Luke also devalues the claims of pedigree by his placement of the family list. It does not occur at the beginning of Luke's narrative, as in Matthew's, but is withheld until chapter 3, after the birth narratives.

7. On the *as* of this text that links the exodus crossing and the Jordan crossing, see Garrett Green, *Imagining God: Theology and the Religious Imagination* (San Francisco: Harper & Row, 1989), 73, 140, who speaks of *as* as the "copula of imagination." That is exactly its function in this text.

8. On such a crucial assessment of this narrative material, see Jay A. Wilcoxen, "Narrative," *Old Testament Form Criticism* (San Antonio, TX: Trinity University Press, 1974), 57–98. Wilcoxen traces the shape of the critical argument from the work of Hermann Gunkel and Hugo Gressmann. I suggest that Wilcoxen's own discussion is illustrative of the stance usually taken by critical scholars. Karl Barth, *Church Dogmatics IV/1* (Edinburgh: T. & T. Clark, 1958), 80–82; and *Church Dogmatics III/2* (Edinburgh: T. & T. Clark, 1960), 441–49, of course, did not succumb to such modern rationality and happily had a very different view of saga and legend as carriers of biblical testimony.

9. These words are from the now widely used emancipatory song from South Africa; see *The New Century Hymnal* (Cleveland: Pilgrim Press, 1995), no. 526.

Chapter 4

TRUTH TRANSFORMS POWER
Josiah

The books of Kings, part of the Deuteronomic history according to dominant hypothesis, traces the long, royal history of Israel and Judah toward its demise. Its culmination in the destruction of Jerusalem in 587 BCE is the target of the entire narrative. The cumulative case built toward that target event is that royal Jerusalem has a long history of disobedience to YHWH's Torah and eventually brings on itself the severe curses that function as sanctions for the enforcement of covenant or, at any rate, as the inescapable consequences for long-term violation of covenant. The case is built by an inventory of disobedient kings who did not trust or obey YHWH in their practice of public power.

Most notorious among these disobedient kings, according to this interpretive report, was Manasseh who had a long reign in Jerusalem (ruled from 687–642 BCE; see

2 Kgs. 21). The verdict on his reign is unusually long and unusually negative:

> He did what was evil in the sight of the LORD, following the abominable practices of the nations that the LORD drove out before the people of Israel. For he rebuilt the high places that his father Hezekiah had destroyed; he erected altars for Baal, made a sacred pole, as King Ahab of Israel had done, worshiped all the host of heaven, and served them. He built altars in the house of the LORD, of which the LORD had said, "In Jerusalem I will put my name." He built altars for all the host of heaven in the two courts of the house of the LORD. He made his son pass through fire; he practiced soothsaying and augury, and dealt with mediums and with wizards. He did much evil in the sight of the LORD, provoking him to anger. The carved images of Asherah that he had made he set in the house of which the LORD had said to David and to his son Solomon, "In this house, and in Jerusalem, which I have chosen out of all the tribes of Israel, I will put my name forever; I will not cause the feet of Israel to wander any more out of the land that I gave to their ancestors, if only they will be careful to do according to all that I have commanded them, and according to all the law that my servant Moses commanded them." But they did not listen; Manasseh misled them to do more evil than the nations had done that the Lord destroyed before the people of Israel. (2 Kgs. 21:2–9)

The outcome of such royal performance is inevitably disaster:

> "Therefore thus says the LORD, the God of Israel, I am bringing on Jerusalem and Judah such evil that the ears of everyone who hears it will tingle. I will stretch over Jerusalem the measuring line of Samaria, and the plummet for the house of Ahab; I will wipe Jerusalem as one wipes a dish, wiping it and turning it upside down. I will cast off

the remnant of my heritage, and give them into the hand of their enemies; they shall become a prey and a spoil to all their enemies." (vv. 12–14)

The decisiveness of Manasseh for the ill fate of Jerusalem is underscored in the subsequent comment:

Still the LORD did not turn from the fierceness of his great wrath, by which his anger was kindled against Judah, because of all the provocations with which Manasseh had provoked him. (2 Kgs. 23:26)

Manasseh figures prominently in the primary story line of Jerusalem and serves the purposes of these historians very well. He would easily be a case study in the way in which power, void of truth, brings deathly trouble.

JOSIAH, THE GOOD KING

My subject, however, is not Manasseh, but his grandson Josiah (ruled from 639–609). He reigned thirty-one years and was thirty-nine years old when he was murdered as a part of a larger political-military intrigue. He looms very large, as we shall see, in this presentation of Israel's history as the good king. Indeed, back in 1963 when John F. Kennedy was assassinated, many of us thought that Kennedy was a parallel to Josiah, staying with the imagery of a king who was young and good. It is beyond the scope of our study, but while we're looking for analogues, it is possible to think that Manasseh, in his long-term destructiveness, was an anticipation of Richard Nixon as he is now commonly judged.

Josiah receives two full chapters in the books of Kings (2 Kgs. 22–23), much more than his grandfather, Manasseh.

And the verdict rendered on him contrasts him completely with his grandfather:

> Before him there was no king like him, who turned to the
> LORD with all his heart, with all his soul, and with all his
> might, according to all the law of Moses; or did any like
> him arise after him. (v. 25)

In what follows I will consider how it was that Josiah received such a positive verdict from the historians and, consequently, what role he played in the larger rendition of Israel's history. I should note at the outset that the historical-critical problems concerning the life and reign of Josiah are acute, because to some extent Josiah is surely a construct of the historians, for he is the ideal embodiment of what the historians most valued, namely, an attentive obeyer of Torah.[1] But then, the critical problems related to Josiah are not greater than they are with the other characters we have considered. In every case, the construal of the lead character is to some extent a matter of constructive imagination, but we can never know to what extent. I mention the matter because in the chronicle-like account of Josiah, we are more likely to be tempted to take the narrative at face value as reportage. I am not naive about this critical problem, but I will proceed to take the text as we have it concerning Josiah as a "model figure," whether as a historical character or to some extent—perhaps to some great extent—as an ideal construct.

I will suggest that either way—as historical character or as ideal construct—Josiah serves well our general reflection on power and truth. As king he exercises real power; but he clearly does so in response to the truth given in Israel's deepest Torah tradition. He functions in the tradition in order to attest that power can serve truth, even as truth can guide, energize, and authorize a particular exercise of power. Thus in Josiah what I have taken as power and as truth converge in his long reign that was against the grain of the story that the historians tell. Apparently the historians bear witness through him to the conviction that it was not inevitable that kings in Jerusalem would contradict Torah. Josiah embodies and exhibits a practice of Torah that did not rely on unconditional Zion theology, but rather adhered to the older covenantal tradition championed by the historians that they judge would have kept Jerusalem safe and secure.

THE SCROLL IN THE TEMPLE

At the center of the Josiah narrative is the report on his temple renovation in chapter 22. Josiah financed temple reform, a sure public gesture of a pious king. But what seems to be an affirmation of the temple becomes, in short order, something quite to the contrary. While rummaging through the temple—that we may imagine had become, in the time of Manasseh, neglected and carelessly disregarded—the workmen find an old scroll. It is like finding an old Bible or a prayer book or angel wings stashed behind the altar, taken to be worthless but without anyone having the authority to discard them. And now the narrative becomes preoccupied with the scroll and is no longer interested in the temple per se.

Hilkiah, the priest, finds the scroll. This priest is not identified, but we can at least note that he has the same name as the father of Jeremiah in Jeremiah 1:1. Jeremiah was a contemporary and close associate of King Josiah, so we are free to speculate about the occurrence of the name of the priest (22:8). Hilkiah the priest takes the scroll to Shaphan, a major political leader who was allied with and in the service of Josiah (v. 8).

Shaphan reads the scroll and promptly takes it to the king (vv. 8, 10). We are not told of Shaphan's response to the scroll, except that he obviously takes it with great seriousness, enough to bring it to the attention of the king. Shaphan reads the scroll to the king; and the king responds to the reading of the scroll with great alarm:

> When the king had the words of the book of the law, he tore his clothes. Then the king commanded the priest Hilkiah, Ahikam son of Shaphan, Achbor son of Micaiah, Shaphan the secretary, and the king's servant Asaiah, saying, "Go, inquire of the LORD for me, for the people, and for all Judah, concerning the words of this book that has been found; for great is the wrath of the LORD that is kindled against us, because our ancestors did not obey the words of this book, to do according to all that is written concerning us." (vv. 11–13)

We should note for future reference that in the report the king tore *(qr')* his garments. That is, Josiah responded with visible, public penitence. He clearly is deeply upset and frightened by the words of the scroll. Most of all to be noted is the fact that the king took the scroll with utmost seriousness, without any royal maneuvering or qualification. He allowed himself as king to be directly addressed by the scroll. We note in passing that, for the moment, the aforementioned temple has disappeared from the narrative. It is all about the scroll!

The king consults with the prophetess Hulda who in response issues an oracle in two parts. In the first part of her oracle, Hulda delivers a standard prophetic speech of judgment with indictment and sentence:

"Thus says the LORD, I will indeed bring disaster on this place and on its inhabitants—all the words of the book that the king of Judah has read. Because they have abandoned me and have made offerings to other gods, so that they have provoked me to anger with all the works of their hands, therefore my wrath will be kindled against this place, and it will not be quenched." (vv. 16–17)

Jerusalem, "this place"—the place of the temple—faces a coming disaster. It is noteworthy that Hulda introduces her oracle by saying, "'Tell the man who sent you to me . . .'" (v. 15). She does not even acknowledge that "the man" is King Josiah. Before prophetic teaching and before the Torah scroll, the king is like every other person, one summoned to obedience. His royal office gains him on points. He cannot save the city or the temple that is under judgment.

The second part of Hulda's oracle is addressed personally to the king:

"But as to the king of Judah, who sent you to inquire of the LORD, thus shall you say to him: Thus says the LORD, the God of Israel: Regarding the words that you have heard, because your heart was penitent, and you humbled yourself before the LORD, when you heard how I spoke against this place, and against its inhabitants, that they should become a desolation and a curse, and because you have *torn* your clothes and wept before me, I also have heard you, says the LORD. Therefore I will gather you to your ancestors, and you shall be gathered to your grave in peace; your eyes shall not see all the disaster that I will bring on this place." (vv. 18–20)[2]

This oracle has the same structure of "because" and "therefore" as the preceding oracle of judgment. Only now the anticipation is positive:

Because Josiah is penitent and humble
Therefore he will die in peace.

Thus the future of Josiah the pious, responsive king, is contrasted to the future of the royal city.

Out of a vigorous response to the scroll and to the words of Hulda, Josiah institutes a great public reform that seeks to bring his regime into sync with the scroll (chapt. 23). Josiah reconstituted the public order of Judah in obedience to the commands of the scroll and in dread of the frightful sanctions voiced in the scroll. His action, it is remembered and reported, constituted a radical departure from the compromised religious practices by that time conventional in the Jerusalem temple. The king attended to the long-standing tension between the radicality of *the covenant and its Torah* and the accommodationist practices of *Jerusalem theology* that had been in vogue since the time of Solomon.

A DEUTERONOMIC FOCUS

It is clear that everything turns on the scroll. And since the historical theologians of the books of Kings are taken to be Deuteronomic, that is, shaped by the book and teaching of Deuteronomy, it does not surprise us that the scroll found that generated the reform is taken, by all interpreters, to be some form of the book of Deuteronomy. Thus Josiah's work in 621 BCE is commonly termed the Deuteronomic reform. Josiah's bold and demanding action fits our theme of power and truth, because the king, as embodiment of royal power, takes the scroll to be the truth and resolves to reorder his power according to that truth. Thus we cannot understand the significance of King Josiah and his reform without attention to the scroll of Deuteronomy. His work was a dazzling example of the way in which power can respond to truth. It strikes me that either the report on Josiah is historically reliable, that Josiah did indeed reshape power by truth, or, if failing that, the historical theologians of 2 Kings wanted to affirm that such a reshaping of power is indeed a real, live, and available choice that powerful people can make.

If we are to think biblically about social responsibility and public policy, then we rightly focus on the book of Deuteronomy that is, in the Bible, the document and tradition that most powerfully transposes the covenant of Sinai into the realm of public practice. Indeed, it is not a stretch to say that Deuteronomy, in its context, became a charter for what we now call liberation theology, namely, the insistence that faith concerns the sustained enactment of public economic justice. We should, in that light, not misread Josiah's purging of religious symbols as a thin, "religious" act (23:4–22). These religious symbols, like all religious symbols, bespeak the arrangement and legitimacy of political-economic power. Thus we may read Josiah's action as a royal resolve to purge not only religious symbols but with them the political-economic arrangement of power that violated the neighborly justice mandated by the scroll of Deuteronomy.

Loving Your Neighbor

For that reason, we must pause to consider the neighborly presuppositions of Deuteronomy that commend love of neighbor as an economic policy and practice.

The book of Deuteronomy commends the "quadrilateral" of the vulnerable in its community: the widow, the orphan, the immigrant, and the poor.[3] These are the ones without conventional protection in a patriarchal society. The argument is that the body politic must protect and sustain the vulnerable who have no other guarantee of protection and sustenance. Very often the focus is on the first three classes of persons—widow, orphan, immigrant—without naming the fourth, the poor. But either way, all the disadvantaged and marginalized are in purview.

–   The scroll protects the vulnerable by limiting the collateral that can be required for loans:

When you make your neighbor a loan of any kind, you shall not go into the house to take the pledge. You shall wait outside, while the person to whom you are making the loan brings the pledge out to you. If the person is poor, you shall not sleep in the garment given you as the pledge. You shall give the pledge back by sunset, so that your neighbor may sleep in the cloak and bless you; and it will be to your credit before the LORD your God (Deut. 24:10–13).

–   The scroll provides that day-laborers must be paid on the day of work. Those who pay cannot withhold payment or simply report that "the check is in the mail":

You shall not withhold the wages of poor and needy laborers, whether other Israelites or aliens who reside in your land in one of your towns. You shall pay them their wages daily before sunset, because they are poor and their livelihood depends on them; otherwise they might cry out to the LORD against you, and you would incur guilt (vv. 14–15).

–   The scroll mandates that the owner-class must not grab up every ounce of produce but must leave some that can be taken and used by the vulnerable. This provision applies precisely to the three money crops of grain, wine, and olive oil:

> When you reap your harvest in the field and forget a sheaf in the field, you shall not go back and get it; it shall be left for the alien, the orphan, and the widow, so that the LORD your God may bless you in all your undertakings. When you beat your olive trees, do not strip what is left; it shall be for the alien, the orphan, and the widow. When you gather the grapes of your vineyard, do not glean what is left; it shall be for the alien, the orphan, and the widow. . . . Remember that you were a slave in the land of Egypt; therefore I am commanding you to do this (vv. 19–20, 22).

This provision in a small agrarian economy amounts to what Frank Cruesemann terms an early "social safety net."[4] The requirement is a recognition that even the vulnerable are legitimate participants in the economy and provision must be made.

Elimination of Debt

At the center of the requirements of the scroll is the provision for "the year of release," the elimination of debt after seven years (Deut. 15:1–18).[5] This teaching requires that at the end of six years, debts that remain unpaid will be cancelled. This most radical teaching intends that the practice of economy shall be subordinated to the well-being of the neighborhood. Social relationships between neighbors— creditors and debtors—are more important and definitional than the economic realities under consideration and there should be no permanent underclass in Israel, so that even the poor are assured wherewithal to participate in the economy in viable ways.

It is impossible to overstate the radicality or importance of this provision that culminates eventually, in Leviticus 25, in the year of jubilee. That is, the scroll is preoccupied with the poor and intends that readers of the scroll—including power-people like the king—should have the poor well in purview as they make and practice economic policy. The urging of the commandment is evident in two statements that seem, at first, to be contradictory. In verse 4, it is affirmed that "There will, however, be no one in need among you" (Deut. 15:4).

That is, obedience to this commandment will lead to the eradication of poverty because being poor is not inevitable but is the outcome of certain economic practices. In verse 11, however, it is stated: "Since there will never cease to be some in need on the earth." This is the statement famously quoted by Jesus in Mark 14:7. It is often read as resigned recognition that the existence of the poor is an irresolvable social reality. That, however, is not the force of verse 11. Rather the recognition of the durable social reality of the poor is an imperative that the cancellation of debts must be continually performed. Thus the *promise* of verse 4 and the *urgency* of verse 11 do not contradict each other. Rather they underscore together the urgency and the effectiveness of the practice.

It is clear in verses 7–9 that the commandment in its radicality evokes resistance from those who found the economic summons too demanding:

> Do not be hard-hearted or tight-fisted toward your needy neighbor. You should rather open your hand, willingly lending enough to meet the need, whatever it may be. Be careful that you do not entertain a mean thought, thinking, "The seventh year, the year of remission, is near," and

therefore view your needy neighbor with hostility and give
nothing; your neighbor might cry out to the LORD against
you, and you would incur guilt. (vv. 7–9)

There were those who were successful in the economy who
did not understand or accept the mandate that the economy must be made to serve the infrastructure of the neighborhood. They preferred to withhold their own economic
resources from the neighborhood and to settle for private
gain and possession. But the commandment is uncompromising and unyielding on the point.

It is for that reason that the commandment utilizes five
instances of the absolute infinitive, a grammatical device
in Hebrew that cannot be recognized in English translation
that intensifies the verb in its urgency. That grammatical
devise strengthens the verb by repeating it in a way that is
unmistakable in Hebrew. Thus:

open-open (v. 8),
lend-lend (v. 8),
give-give (v. 10),
open-open (v. 11),
provide-provide (v. 14).

The best that an English translation can do is to use a
strengthening adverb. The infinitive absolute is not common
in Hebrew rhetoric; thus the use of five of them here indicates the passion with which the point is made.

The concluding reference to the exodus in verse 15 (as
in Deut. 24:22) is an effort to connect the mandate to the
emancipatory tradition of the exodus and to show that Israel
is summoned to an emancipatory economic practice. We
may imagine that these intense cadences of neighborliness

sounded in the ears of Josiah. The teaching made clear to the king that the Jerusalem establishment had lost its way about *the religious symbol system* it relied on, which validated *economic practices* that were harmful and exploitative in the service of the urban elites who clustered around king and temple. Thus we can imagine that in some sense Josiah was a traitor to his class in taking the truth of the scroll as an impetus for the transformation of royal power.

The Threat of Covenantal Curses

The urgency with which Josiah responded to the scroll is most likely rooted in the recital of blessings and curses in Deuteronomy 28. Thus Hulda grounds her announcement of coming disaster on Jerusalem in "all the words of the book that the King of Judah has read" (2 Kgs. 22:16). In Deuteronomy 28:1–14 there is a recital of blessings for Israel when it obeys Torah commandments. The blessings concern a full and abundant life for a Torah-keeping community. But in verses 15–68 the inventory of curses is disproportionately long and harsh. The text asserts that when the Torah is violated, every imaginable evil will come on the community. This is the recurring burden of the prophets who announce the covenantal sanctions that are about to be enacted on disobedient Israel. And it is the pivot point of Hulda's declaration of coming "disaster" (v. 16) that links with Josiah's initial sense that "the wrath of the LORD that is kindled against us" (v. 13).

Thus Josiah's urgent and forceful response to the scroll and the ominous words of Hulda both arise out of this voiced threat of the covenantal curse. The response of the king is in order to avoid the coming disaster. We might have wished that Josiah's motivation had been positive and affirmative. But that is not what we have. We may find such a threat and response to the threat unattractive, because it sounds like a primitive supernaturalism in which God will lash out at a people that displeases God. If, however, we are able to see that the tradition of Deuteronomy is in fact making a much more sophisticated argument, we may be appreciative of the responses of Josiah and Hulda. The tradition of Deuteronomy may be read, instead of repugnant primitivism, as an insistence that the world is morally coherent, that deeds and policies have consequences, and that future possibilities for the community grow out of present choices and policy decisions. The rhetoric of divine judgment is an insistence that there is a deep and nonnegotiable answerability to the public process. And King Josiah understood that clearly.

Such a theology, deeply rooted in Sinai, flies in the face of Jerusalem theology in which Josiah's regime was ensconced. That theology—centered in dynasty and temple—focused on David as chosen king and Jerusalem as chosen city, and claimed that king, city, and temple are given abiding guarantees of unconditional divine support and are therefore immune to moral accountability. Such a theology will most likely lead to a self-indulgent complacency; that was the case in Jerusalem.

Thus the moment of scroll reading in the regime of Josiah constituted a most profound contestation between competing theologies: that of *the Jerusalem establishment* that enjoyed power and that of *the old covenantal tradition* that summoned accountability. It is utterly remarkable that Josiah immediately understood what was at stake. He promptly embraced the truth of the scroll and understood that his claim on power had to submit to that truth.

We may thus understand his response in reform as an effort to reconstitute his government and his power on the basis of the truthful scroll of covenant. Josiah, in his immediate context, discerned the danger into which his regime had fallen due to the covenantal indifference of the dynasty and reflected by the reign of Manasseh. He moved to correct the blatant realities of Torah disobedience in Jerusalem:

- He established a covenant in the public domain:

  > The king stood by the pillar and made a covenant before the LORD, to follow the LORD, keeping his commandments, his decrees, and his statutes, with all his heart and all his soul, to perform the words of this covenant that were written in this book. (23:3)

- In verses 4–20, 24, the king removed all the totems and icons of noncovenantal, non-Yahwistic worship:

  > The king commanded . . . to bring out of the temple of the Lord all the vessels made for Baal, for Asherah, and for all the host of heaven; he burned them outside Jerusalem in the fields of the Kidron, and carried their ashes to Bethel. (v. 4)

- The king reconstituted the celebration of Passover, as he led the populace back to the fundamental traditions of the exodus and Sinai (vv. 21–23).

We may also see why these historical theologians center their work on his reform; they believe that the truth of Israel's history is deeply given in that covenantal truthfulness in which no dimension of unconditional chosenness or exceptionalism can supersede or void. Thus Josiah performs in a dramatic way the conviction of these narrative interpreters who insist that the old covenantal realities pertain and that no amount of urban sophistication or clever theological maneuvering can gainsay that reality. Thus the covenant that Josiah made in 2 Kings 23:2, the purging of false religious symbols (vv. 4–14), and the reconstitution of the Passover (vv. 21–23) are facets of deep reorientation. It is no wonder that Josiah received the remarkable verdict for his courageous embrace of truth:

> Before him there was no king like him, who turned to the Lord with all his heart, with all his soul, and with all his might, according to all the law of Moses; nor did any like him arise after him. (v. 25)

One can recognize the cadences of Deuteronomy in this formulation. Josiah responds with heart, soul, and mind, that is, with all his capacity in socio-economic, political policy. He embraces the Torah of Moses as given in the book of Deuteronomy. He turned to YHWH, a turning that required a redeployment of power. The historians know the outcome of the matter. They know that after Josiah things went from bad to worse and eventually to destruction. They know that even the courage of Josiah was not enough. And so they follow their generous verdict on Josiah in the next verse with "Still" (or perhaps one might translate with a stronger adversative, "Yet" or "Nevertheless," or as one might say in German, "Doch!"):

> Still the Lord did not turn from the fierceness of his great wrath, by which his anger was kindled against Judah, because of all the provocations with which Manasseh had provoked him. (v. 26)

The old illusion of exceptionalism prevailed! In the end, the power arrangement in Jerusalem did not and could not prevail. Better to have followed the path of Josiah! But then, power rarely follows the path of scroll-obedience. And so Josiah is reckoned by the historians as an interlude in Israel's determined march toward death, an interlude that bore witness to what is possible and what might have been. What might have been is the kind of fidelity that bends socio-economic and political power toward the neighbor. As a model, Josiah is the counterpoint to Elisha. As we have seen, Elisha disregarded the kings and performed his own peculiar counter-history. Josiah, however, is cast as a player in the dominant history; he cannot disregard royal reality. He permits the conviction that public policy and the public infrastructure can be transformed when the scroll and its counterproposal is taken seriously. From Josiah we are invited to pay more attention to the scroll and its truth.

THE SCROLL SPEAKS TO POWER

I want now to further extrapolate concerning Josiah by drawing his testimony out toward three other texts. First I ask, did Josiah have to heed the scroll? I answer by reference to his son Jehoiakim (2 Kgs. 23:36–24:7), a king reckoned, in contrast to Josiah, as one who did evil in the sight of the Lord.

The prophet Jeremiah who has very close links to the tradition of Deuteronomy was active in the days of Jehoiakim. In Jeremiah 36 it is reported that Jeremiah—"in the fourth year of King Jehoiakim" (v. 1), that is, in 605 BCE, at the behest of YHWH—dictated a scroll to his secretary, Baruch. This act of dictation is commonly taken to be the point of origin of what became the book (scroll) of Jeremiah. Because Jeremiah is persona non grata to the regime of Jehoiakim, he dispatches Baruch to read his words from the scroll in public. Baruch reads the scroll "in the hearing of all the people of Judah" (v. 6). We are told that he read it in "the chamber of Gamariah, son of Shaphan, the secretary, which was in the upper court, at the entry of the New Gate of the LORD's house" (v. 10).

This was perhaps a second reading, for reading in such a room is not "in the hearing of all the people." His reading of the scroll was promptly reported to the authorities, as though the public domain was under acute surveillance, likely reflecting the anxiety of the regime. Thus Baruch reads the scroll a second time (or a third time?), this time in the cabinet room (v. 15). The high officials who heard the scroll decided that the king must get a report on this lethal document from Jeremiah. But first they interrogated Baruch about the origin of the document. The exchange is a curious one, because when Baruch told them that Jeremiah himself had dictated the scroll, they advised him: "'Go and hide, you and Jeremiah, and let no one know where you are'" (v. 19).

It is as though these officials knew that these words of Jeremiah's scroll were dangerous and inflammatory. More than that, they were in sympathy with the gist of the argument. We know that Jeremiah's scroll reflected the old covenantal tradition of Sinai, relayed by Deuteronomy. And we know that the royal establishment in Jerusalem—except for Josiah—had completely disregarded that tradition. But here are officials, high in the service of the king, who empathize with this presentation. This means that they secretly and carefully resisted the king's policies. And so they are ready to protect Baruch and Jeremiah; they urged them to go into hiding because they knew that those who birthed the scroll would be at risk.

They brought the scroll to the king for they knew that the scroll of Jeremiah would say some things that the king needed to hear that they had not the courage or the freedom to say. And so, in a very dramatic scene, the scribe reads the scroll of Jeremiah to the king. The king listens. And then,

> Now the king was sitting in his winter apartment (it was the ninth month), and there was a fire burning in the brazier before him. As Jehudi read three or four columns, the king would cut them off with a penknife and throw them into the fire in the brazier, until the entire scroll was consumed in the fire that was in the brazier. (vv. 22-23)

The narrative adds that the royal entourage was so enwrapped in its ideology that it was not alarmed by the scroll of Jeremiah. The reading did not evoke alarm or any acts of penitent response: "Yet neither the king, nor any of his servants who heard all these words, was alarmed, nor did they tear their garments" (v. 24).

Some in the room urged the king not to burn the scroll because they knew it was important. But to no avail: "Even when Elnathan and Deliaiah and Gemariah urged the king not to burn the scroll he would not listen to them" (v. 25).

The king in fact not only burned the scroll in order to eliminate this truth-telling witness to covenant; he organized a posse to hunt down the two subversives in order to silence them. That is, the king shredded the documents in order to dismiss the truth-telling and then sought to eliminate the truth-tellers. The narrative adds laconically: "But the LORD hid them" (v. 26).

Of course! Except that we must know enough to connect this terse report in verse 26 with the advice of verse 19. It was the Lord who hid them; but it was the officialdom of Jerusalem that took steps to protect them from royal wrath. In the paragraph of sequel, YHWH, via Jeremiah, announces a severe threat against the king because he burned the scroll:

You have dared to burn this scroll, saying, Why have you written in it that the king of Babylon will certainly come and destroy this land, and will cut off from it human beings and animals? Therefore thus says the LORD concerning King Jehoiakim of Judah: He shall have no one to sit upon the throne of David, and his dead body shall be cast out to the heat by day and frost by night. And I will punish him and his offspring and his servants for their iniquity; I will bring on them, and on the inhabitants of Jerusalem and on the people of Judah, all the disasters with which I have threatened them—but they would not listen. (vv. 29-31)

TO TEAR—A DESTRUCTIVE
AND PROTECTIVE FORCE

My focus in these extracts is on the use of the verb *tear* in verses 23-24: "the king would cut them off with a penknife. . . . Yet neither the king, nor any of his servants who heard all these words, was alarmed, nor did they tear their garments." The first usage of our verb is translated "cut," but it is the same verb that is later translated to "tear" *(qr')*. In verse 24, it is observed that the king did not tear his clothes in response to the scroll.

Ernest Nicholson has noticed that the double use of the term "tear" in this chapter is the same term used in the report of Josiah when he heard the scroll of Deuteronomy in 2 Kings 22: 11: "When the king heard the words of the book of the law, he *tore* his clothes." And in v. 19 Josiah is commended for his penitence: "Because you have *torn* your clothes and wept before me." Josiah tore his clothes. Jehoiakim, his son, *tore* (cut) the scroll, but not his garments. Nicholson comments on this contrast:

The narrative in question was consciously composed as a parallel to 2 Kings xxii, with the primary intention of pointing to the contrast between the reaction of Jehoiakim to the Word of God and that of his revered father Josiah whose humble obedience to the Book of the Law and the reformation which he carried out in response to its demand are recorded. . . . There appears to be a very deliberate contrast drawn between Josiah's penitence on hearing the Book of the Law and Jehoiakim's attitude and reaction to Jeremiah's scroll.[6]

Nicholson adds in a footnote:

This suggests that the authors of the narrative are deliberately contrasting groups involved in the events recorded, on the one hand the "Josian" officials and on the other hand the king and his "servants." . . . This contrast is further evidenced by that drawn between those who wished to destroy the scroll and those who wished to preserve it (vv. 20, 23, 25) as also between those who attempted to arrest and (probably) execute prophet and those who sought to protect him (vv. 19, 26).[7]

Now my purpose is not to spend too much time on Jehoiakim and his entourage that resisted the scroll of Jeremiah with its truth-telling about the Jerusalem operation. That is clear enough. What interests me is that Josiah is an exception to the royal rule. Characteristically, kings would not welcome the old scroll and its covenantal vision of Israel. They surely did not welcome prophetic testimony concerning the contemporaneity of the old covenantal traditions. They did not want to hear about the old, rooted divine purpose that curbed royal ambition and that testified against royal self-indulgence. It is hardly news that kings resist the old tradition of limit.

All the more reason to marvel at Josiah, for he did not need to heed the scroll. He did not need to be alarmed. He did not need to tear his garments in penitence. He did not need to institute a great reform. He did not need to depart at all from the "ways of the king" that, since 1 Samuel 8:11, have been ways of confiscation and usurpation. But he did! For that reason he embodies an astonishing exception in ancient Israel of a power agent who responded to covenantal truth, who insisted that public policy must cohere with the covenantal traditions of love of neighbor.

Thus we may posit a counterforce among the Jerusalem elites who took critical distance from the conventional exceptionalism of Jerusalem ideology. This company of counterforce included the king, along with Jeremiah who himself provided a scroll, and Baruch who came from a distinguished family of scribes. It also included public officials who knew that royal policy was foolish, the ones who wanted to protect Jeremiah and Baruch, among them Shaphan and his powerful political family. Nicholson says of this little group:

> In view of the sympathy which members of the house of Shaphan are described elsewhere in the book of Jeremiah (xxvi, 24, xxix, 3) as having shown to Jeremiah, it is possible that they had remained loyal to the principles of the Deuteronomic reformation carried out by Josiah and because of this were well disposed toward the prophet. . . . It need indicate no more than that the house of Shaphan, because of its attachment to the theology of the Deuteronomic circle with its intense interest in prophecy, acknowledged the divine authority of the word which Jeremiah spoke.[8]

Such a map of the two groups in Jerusalem suggests that the Deuteronomic advocates against royal policy included not simply the invisible scroll people and/or the prophet but also a sober, formidable political body that understood that power cannot finally be administered in arbitrary or self-serving ways. They knew, from rootage in the tradition, that such absolutizing power against the neighbor is destructive and that the historical process, governed by God, with its intransigent moral dimension, will press energy against such willfulness. When one does such a critique of power in Jerusalem, the choices made by Josiah are all the more significant.

CONTRASTING JOSIAH AND JEHOIAKIM

On that basis we may focus on a reflection of Jeremiah concerning Josiah, for clearly the scrolls of Deuteronomy and Jeremiah are intimately connected. In Jeremiah 22:13–18, the poet offers a critique of and lament over King Jehoiakim who had so vigorously opposed him. The poem begins, as is characteristic in prophetic polemic, with a "woe" of coming trouble:

> Woe to him who builds his house by unrighteousness,
>   and his upper rooms by injustice;
> who makes his neighbors work for nothing,
>   and does not give them their wages;
> who says, "I will build myself a spacious house
>   with large upper rooms,"
> and who cuts out windows for it,
>   paneling it with cedar,
>   and painting it with vermillion.
>
> (vv. 13–14)

The king is indicted by standards of the old covenant, for policies and practices of *unrighteousness* and *injustice,* that is, for exploitation of the neighbor. Specifically the charge is exploitative labor practices, a labor policy modeled after Solomon and known in Israel already since Pharaoh. The need for cheap labor is due to royal extravagance concerning an upper story, windows, and cedar in the palace. The tradition knows that the underside of such excess extravagance is always cheap labor that of necessity violates the neighbor.

The indictment of the king continues in verse 17 with a charge of violence, oppression, and dishonest gain:

> But your eyes and heart
>   are only on your dishonest gain,
> for shedding innocent blood,
>   and for practicing oppression and violence.
>   (v. 17)

And then, with a vigorous rhetorical "therefore," the poet draws the inescapable consequence of a dishonorable death for the king:

> They shall not lament for him, saying,
>   "Alas, my brother!" or "Alas, sister!"
> They shall not lament for him, saying,
>   "Alas, lord!" or "Alas, his majesty!"
> With the burial of a donkey he shall be buried—
>   dragged off and thrown out beyond the gates
>   of Jerusalem.
>   (vv. 18–19)

In this poetic anticipation, the king will not be honored at death but will be disposed of in ignoble ways. When I read this, I think of the bloody body of the hated dictator in Romania up against the wall or, earlier, the hanging body of Mussolini in the streets of Rome. Such obdurate power, says the poet, will come to an end in shame and humiliation.

What interests us here, however, is that right in the midst of this rhetorical disposal of Jehoiakim, the invective is interrupted for two verses on the father of Jehoiakim, namely, Josiah. These two verses take King Josiah as a complete contrast to his son who is here condemned:

Did not your father eat and drink
and do justice and righteousness?
Then it was well with him.
He judged the cause of the poor and needy;
Then it was well.
Is not this to know me?
says the LORD.

(vv. 15–16)

The father of Jehoiakim, Josiah, did *justice and righteousness*. The two terms on neighborly solidarity have their negative counterpoint in verse 13 concerning Jehoiakim, *injustice and unrighteousness*. And Josiah prospered because he lived according to the old covenant tradition: "It was well with him." He received the old covenantal blessing of *shalom* because he lived by the old covenantal requirements. He accepted those covenantal requirements as the guide for his governance.

And then the poet goes on to itemize this royal justice and righteousness; it comes down to this. He "judged" the cause of the poor and the needy, that is, he intervened on their behalf. He made his government a vehicle for the protection and sustenance of the vulnerable:

To judge the cause of the poor and needy under Josiah's reign (v. 16a) was to see that they did not suffer abuse, that their labor did not go uncompensated, that their property was not extorted from them, that the legal system was not manipulated by bribery and other devices to rob those who did not have much in the first place. Jehoiakim failed the test of kingship in every way.[9]

That commitment is the ground of *shalom,* according to this tradition.

And then the poem adds a most remarkable reflection on the reality of YHWH: "Is this not to know me?" The statement equates justice toward the poor with knowledge of God! It is not that justice leads to such knowledge or that such knowledge of God leads to justice. Rather the two are the same! Jose Miranda takes the testimony of 1 John 4 as a riff on Jeremiah 22:15–16:

> Let us return to John. It is of this love that 1 John 4:7–8 affirms that he who loves his neighbor knows God and he who does not love his neighbor does not know God. This is exactly the decisive teaching of Jer. 22:16 and of all the prophets. And just as in this teaching we find the deepest reason for the anticultus of the prophets, in the same way John uses this thesis as the basis for his rejection of all "direct" access to God.[10]

Miranda then quotes I John 4:12, 16, 20, and 7–8 in that order. This daring linkage between the holy God of covenant and the needy neighbor is a linkage insisted on in the Sinai covenant that in Christian tradition comes to expression in the lyrical formulation of creedal Christology, "truly divine, truly human." But before Christian tradition, the prophetic tradition of Israel saw the defining linkage clearly:

> For thus says the high and lofty one
>   who inhabits eternity, whose name is Holy;
> I dwell in the high and lofty place,
>   and also with those who are contrite and humble
>   in spirit,
> to revive the spirit of the humble.
>   (Isa. 57:15)

The God of covenant is holy and inhabits eternity with the humble and contrite. In the grammar of that sentence, the two residences of God are completely parallel, governed by the single verb, *skn*, which means "sojourn, dwell provisionally." Josiah knew this and ordered his power in such a way. By contrast, Jehoiakim and his entourage assumed that if one could eliminate the scroll, one could break this linkage and have *the high God* without *the lowly neighbor.*

But of course, one cannot finally beat the scroll. For it is written at the end of Jeremiah 36 that Jeremiah redictated the scroll to Baruch, "and many similar words were added" (Jer. 36:32). Truth is not disposed of, even when resisted by power. The scroll keeps coming at us with its truth!

THE ROYAL PSALMS MANDATE JUSTICE

We may ask, before we finish, how did Josiah know this about God and neighbor? He surely was surrounded by all sorts of seductions that wanted him not to know it. I submit that he knew it because the liturgy, even the royal liturgy in the Solomonic temple, attested to this truth.[11] The great enthronement psalms that kings must surely have loved attested the commitment of God to justice and righteousness:

> He will judge the world with *righteousness,*
>   and the peoples with his *truth.*
> (Ps. 96:13)

> He will judge the world with *righteousness,*
>   and the peoples with *equity.*
> (Ps. 98:9)

But it is especially Psalm 99 in this group of psalms that makes the case:

Mighty king, *lover of justice*,
   you have established *equity*;
you have executed *justice*
   and *righteousness* in Jacob.
                    (v. 4)

YHWH is a lover of justice! YHWH has established justice! YHWH executed justice and righteousness. These are the mantras of prophetic poetry that are rooted in old covenantal tradition. But now it is in the royal liturgy!

And above all, Psalm 72, a royal Psalm, connects such policies of socio-economic justice to the well-being of the king. The Psalm makes the same connection as the verses in Jeremiah 22 concerning justice and wellness. The Psalm begins with the same pair of terms we have found in Jeremiah 22 concerning both Jehoiakim and Josiah:

Give the king your *justice*, O God
   and your *righteousness* to a king's son.
                    (v. 1)

That practice of justice and righteousness enjoined the king as governor more specifically in what follows:

May he judge your people with righteousness,
   and your poor with justice.
. . . .
May he defend the cause of the poor of the people,
   give deliverance to the needy,
   and crush the oppressor.
. . . .
For he delivers the needy when they call,
   the poor and those who have no helper.
He has pity on the weak and the needy,
   and saves the lives of the needy.
From oppression and violence he redeems their life;
   and precious is their blood in his sight.
                    (vv. 2, 4, 12–14)

The brief of the king is protection and sustenance of the vulnerable, with particular reference to the economy.

The repeated counterpoint in the Psalm is that a king who has such policies will prosper and be blessed in every way (vv. 5–6, 8–11, and 15–17). This extravagant language of *shalom* imagines every possible dimension of royal well-being. The specificity of the poetry may indeed recall Solomon's well-being with particular reference to Tarshish, Sheba, and Seba (vv. 10, 15). Solomon is ironically the "gold standard" for well-being. I use the phrase to indicate both that Solomon dominated the use of money and that his practice was normative for measures of wealth. Specifically verse 7 of the Psalm anticipates that such a king will not only live long and well but will be marked by righteousness that eventuates in total well-being (*shalom*):

> In his days may righteousness flourish
>   and peace abound, until the moon is no more.

Thus the Psalm, by its counterpoint of *mandate* and *assurance*, makes the linkage of justice and well-being. Even the royal liturgy articulates the connection that power (royal power) must attend to the truth of the neighbor in order to prosper. The remarkable connection that interrupts the hubris of royal power is reinforced by the belated superscription of the Psalm, "Of Solomon" (v. 1). Given our earlier discussion of Solomon, I can only think that this superscription may be taken ironically, that Solomon is recalled as the failed king who defaulted on this defining connection.

Thus I dare to imagine that Josiah was an attentive child of the liturgy. He may, in ways we do not know, have been schooled in the tradition of Deuteronomy, thus a late parallel to King Joash who was nurtured by the priest Jehoida in the ways of covenant (2 Kgs. 10:4–12, 17–20; see 2 Chr. 23:8–24:27). Beyond that, however, my point is that the king must have been regularly exposed to the liturgical recital. And he took it seriously! He believed it and responded to it. The reason that this is important for us is that in our contemporary life, power-people are regularly exposed to liturgical affirmation of the same truth. The claims are everywhere in our most familiar liturgical life. But power-people—all of us, like the ancient kings—are so inured in the ideology of exceptionalism that the claims do not penetrate. We may imagine that the reason Josiah is such an exception to the royal rule is that he leapt beyond the ideology of exceptionalism to the truth of neighborly covenant. It is exactly the truth of neighborly covenant, vouched for in the scroll tradition, that convicts or subverts every conventional exceptionalism. Josiah's dread and alarm and his tearing of his garments constitute a recognition that the claims of the old tradition, even if they are too familiarly recited, are in fact serious and ominous. He acted with his power in response to the truth that addressed him.

THE STORY OF JOSIAH:
READING AS CONTESTANTS

Before I finish, I'll make one suggestion as I have in each case study, of the way in which this particular reading of truth and power is evidenced in New Testament testimony. I suggest that Josiah's attentiveness to the "poor and needy" (Jer. 22:15–16), rooted in covenantal mandate and enacted in royal policy, has an important echo in the parable of Jesus in Matthew 25:31–46. The parable turns on the affirmation that attentiveness to Christ takes the form of attentiveness to the least:

The radical shock is that the concern of Jesus was hidden in the sick, the hungry, the thirsty, the naked, and the imprisoned. They are not only the "brothers" of Jesus; Jesus identified with them. The "just" are not just because they acted out of conscious Christological motivation, but simply because they cared for the "least." The answer to their question, "When did we see thee?" is implicitly, When we saw the least. But "seeing" itself is not enough. It was "seeing" translated into effective care which made the first group blessed; "seeing" alone brought condemnation to the second group.[12]

By linking "the least" to the rule of Christ, the Matthew tradition continues the trajectory we have already seen whereby power authorized by God is shaped by the truth of the needy neighbor.

John Donahue offers a thorough discussion concerning this disruptive identity of the least. In popular usage, the parable receives a "universal" interpretation, that the least of all are the needy:

People will be called "just" and "blessed" on the basis of actions done simply for any person in need. This understanding has been underscored by contemporary theologies of liberation. The praxis of justice, seen as concern for the marginal in society, rather than cult or creed, constitutes true religion, which is not limited to those who confess Jesus as "Lord."[13]

But Donahue himself avers that in the original telling, the "least" are abused and needy Christian missionaries:

The Matthean church is to be a community in mission that will bear witness to the "gospel of the kingdom" in the awareness that they will face rejection and persecution. The identity of the least of the brothers and sisters of Jesus in Matt. 25:31-46 and their specific sufferings are to be interpreted from this perspective. The sufferings borne by the least of the brothers and sisters of Jesus are apostolic sufferings borne in proclaiming the gospel.[14]

It may well be that in context the teaching of Jeremiah 22:15–16 and the liturgical affirmation of Psalm 72 had a like limitation concerning the poor and needy who were precisely in the purview of royal policy. Be that as it may, we are not disobedient to the parable itself if we parse the identification made in the parable between Christ and the least. That identification is a precise echo of "Is this not to know me?" in Jeremiah. That radicality in ancient Israel surely confounded those who celebrated God amid the splendor of the temple. In like manner it must have confounded Jesus' opponents to identify Christ with the least of any ilk.

It would (and does) require such radical theological identification in order to draw power into the orbit of truth. Terry Eagleton, in his answer to the new atheists (Dawkins and Hitchens) concerning the truth of faith, does not argue on philosophical or theoretical grounds. Rather he focuses on praxis wherein Jesus identified with and stands in solidarity with the "scum of the earth":

> The only authentic image of this violently loving God is a tortured and executed political criminal, who dies in an act of solidarity with what the Bible calls the *anawim*, meaning the destitute and dispossessed. Crucifixion was saved by the Romans for political offenses alone. The *anawim*, in Pauline phrase, are the shit of the earth—the scum and refuse of society who constitute the cornerstone of the new form of human life known as the kingdom of God. Jesus himself is consistently presented as their representative.[15]

In his robust and entertaining way Eagleton shows how the teaching and life of Jesus appeared to be absurd to the dominant culture, and by that absurdity exposed the genuine absurdity of dominant culture in its illusionary posturing. His brilliant, defiant rhetoric observes how this radicality in our time clashes with the dominant reason of the U.S. government ("Washington D.C.") and of the common room of the academy (with "Oxford").

> I am not foolish enough to imagine for a moment that Ditchkins would be impressed with the theological account I have given, since for one thing it is scarcely the conventional wisdom of North Oxford or Washington D.C. It represents a view of human condition that is far more radical than anything Richard Dawkins is likely to countenance, with his eminently suburban, smugly sanguine trust in the efficacy of a spot of social engineering here and dose of liberal enlightenment there . . . The view of the world I have just laid out is not what one characteristically hears around North Oxford dinner tables or in the fleshpots of the U. S. capital.[16]

The parallels are poignant. It is, of course, a ready risk to read too much back in to Josiah and to imagine more about him than is warranted. Nonetheless, he stands in the tradition as a reminder of what is possible, or at least what is imaginable. He is remembered as the embodiment of power that is vigorously different, contrasting with usual royal power of which Ezekiel has written:

> Ah, you shepherds of Israel who have been feeding yourselves! Should not shepherds feed the sheep? You eat the fat, you clothe yourselves with the wool, you slaughter the fatlings; but you do not feed the sheep. You have not strengthened the weak, you have not healed the sick, you have not bound up the injured, you have not brought back the strayed, you have not sought the lost, but with force and harshness you have ruled them. So they were scattered, because there was no shepherd. (Ezek. 34:2–5)

In our time we know about being scattered in anxiety and violence. Josiah stands as a reminder that it could have been otherwise among us. Indeed, it still could be otherwise!

NOTES

1. Richard Nelson, "Josiah in the Book of Joshua," *Journal of Biblical Literature* 100 (1981): 531–40, has shown the way in which Joshua, in the book of Joshua, is constructed as a counterpoint to Josiah at the end of the corpus, as both are model advocates and practitioners of Torah. On page 540, Nelson terms Joshua "a thinly disguised Josianic figure."

2. There is an awkwardness in the tradition because this promise of a peaceable death for the king is contradicted by the reported fact of his murder; see Stanley Brice Frost, "The Death of Josiah: A Conspiracy of Silence," *Journal of Biblical Literature* 87 (1968): 369–82.

3. I take this phrase of "the quartette of the vulnerable" from Nicholas Wolterstorff, *Justice: Rights and Wrongs* (Princeton, NJ: Princeton University Press, 2008), 75–82.

4. Frank Cruesemann, *The Torah: Theology and Social History of Old Testament Law* (Edinburgh: T. & T. Clark, 1996), 224–34.

5. See Jeffries M. Hamilton, *Social Justice and Deuteronomy: The Case of Deuteronomy 15* (Dissertation Series 136; Atlanta: Scholars Press, 1992), and more broadly, Moshe Weinfeld, *Social Justice in Ancient Israel and in the Ancient Near East* (Minneapolis: Fortress Press, 1995).

6. Ernest W. Nicholson, *Preaching to the Exiles: A Study of the Prose Tradition in the Book of Jeremiah* (Oxford: Blackwell, 1970), 42-43.

7. Ibid., 44 n. 2.

8. Ibid.

9. Patrick D. Miller, "The Book of Jeremiah," *New Interpreter's Bible* 6 (Nashville: Abingdon Press, 2001), 742.

10. Jose Miranda, *Marx and the Bible: A Critique of the Philosophy of Oppression* (Maryknoll, NY: Orbis Books, 1974), 63–64.

11. For a very positive estimate of Zion (temple) theology, see Ben C. Ollenburger, *Zion, the City of the Great King: A Theological*

Symbol of the Jerusalem Cult (*JSOT* Supp. 41; Sheffield: JSOT Press, 1987).

12. Jon Donahue, *The Gospel in Parables: Metaphor, Narrative, and Theology in the Synoptic Gospels* (Philadelphia: Fortress Press, 1988), 113.

13. Ibid., 110.

14. Ibid., 122.

15. Terry Eagleton, *Reason, Faith, and Revolution: Reflections on the God Debate* (New Haven, CT: Yale University Press, 2009), 23.

16. Ibid., 34-35

Chapter 5

POWER AND TRUTH AMONG US

I<small>T HAS BEEN MY PURPOSE IN THESE EXPLORATIONS TO EXHIBIT</small>
some of the different ways in which the Bible articulates
the complex interface of power and truth. It is evident that
the interpretive, imaginative agility of the biblical tradition
follows no settled formulation of that interface because it
is always immediately contextual and cannot be reduced
to a formula. Nor it is possible to work out a grid or taxonomy of options, as perhaps Richard Niebuhr has offered,
because the Bible proceeds by narrative particularity. One
cannot generalize from narrative, though that is our endless
temptation. One can only tell the narrative again, each time
with yet another act of interpretive imagination.

TRUTH SUBVERTS POWER FROM BELOW

Power, whenever and wherever it can, will present itself as a totalizing system, the wishful thinking of every empire, every regime, and every orthodoxy. Such totalizing claims, as best they can, answer all questions, provide all resources, guarantee all futures, and deny the possibility that anything meaningful or valuable can fall outside of the totalizing ideology. It is fair to see that very claim on the horizon of ancient Israel. At the very outset Pharaoh represents such an attempt at totality. And within Israel, Solomon embodied the same attempt as his Egyptian father-in-law.[1]

At a minimum, truth is the sneaky whisper and the resilient reminder that the totalizing claim of the regime is not true. There always falls outside the capacity of the regime the irreducible voice of pain that is inescapably and always a voice of hope that refuses the imposed silence of the regime. That minimal whisper outside the totality is initially voiced in the Bible through the cry of the slaves (Exod. 2:23). But the Bible attests that the minimal whisper of pain and hope is transposed into something maximal. It is transposed by affirming that what lies outside the claim of the regime is not only the cry of pain and hope but the answering faithful engagement of the Holy One who intrudes into and shatters the claim of that totality. Thus the uncompromising holiness of God comes to historical articulation and enactment in a way that summons power to answer, the very power that thought there was none to whom answer must be given.[2] Thus at the end of the dramatic deconstruction of Pharaoh's power in the exodus narrative—after Pharaoh has exercised his immense power and given free voice to his rage at the slave challenge—Pharaoh must finally speak in a supplicating voice to Moses: "'Take your flocks and your herds, as you said, and be gone. And bring a blessing on me too!'" (Exod. 12:32). In this request to be blessed, it has become clear, even to the empire, that the capacity to generate a future is denied Pharaoh and indwells the movement of Moses.

It is not a straight line, but it is a traceable line that runs all the way from the pathos-filled plea of Pharaoh to the bewildered query of Pilate, "What is truth?" (John 18:38). In that stunning moment of bewildered query, the power of Rome has come to recognize the inadequacy and failure of its totalizing claims. One can say, readily enough, that the subverting force of truth that breaks this absolutizing power is from below. Of course! It always is! But it is also more than from below, if that phrase simply refers to the powerless and marginal. For as biblical tradition attests, it is also allied with the elusive, resilient, resolved power of the holy God. Thus it is Moses . . . dispatched by YHWH (Exod. 3:10). Moses does not say, "Let my people go." He says, rather, "*Thus says YHWH*, 'Let my people go'" (Exod. 5:1, au. trans.). And in like fashion, Solomon is interrupted by the deconstructive shrewdness of irony and finally by the embodied action of Ahijah, the Shilonite, who will, at the behest of YHWH, tear the tribes away from the throne of David (1 Kgs. 11:29–31). The action is by Ahijah, but it is the purpose of YHWH that presides in the declaration:

> He then said to Jeroboam: Take for yourself ten pieces; for thus says the LORD, the God of Israel, "See, I am about to tear the kingdom from the hand of Solomon, and will give you ten tribes." (v. 31)

And even with Josiah it is the commanding voice of the scroll that summons. Thus the biblical narrative, in a variety of ways, gives dramatic form to the elusive power of God. That sustained attestation concerning the resolve of YHWH never yields in its conviction that power is put on notice by such truthfulness. That truth is not a cognitive package; it is a deep practical awareness that the force of emancipation will not be resisted (Moses); the hunger of many vulnerable folk will be heard and honored, the royal famine notwithstanding (Elisha); the bureaucratic power of visible authority cannot be maintained in the face of agitation from below (Solomon); and the dread sanctions of Torah cannot be eluded or outflanked (Josiah).

OLD TESTAMENT TRUTH SPEAKS TO NEW TESTAMENT POWER

I have been preoccupied with the Old Testament, both because that is my interest and competence and because the interface of power and truth is made dramatically front and center in the narrative witness of that tradition. But I have also suggested, in each case, how these narrative episodes from ancient Israel can be readily and faithfully carried into the New Testament and into the church's witness to Jesus as the Messiah. Thus current scholarly awareness is that the faith community of the New Testament lived at an interface with the Roman Empire and with the Jewish leaders who colluded with the imperial power of Rome.[3] That awareness makes it easy enough to see, unmistakably see, that the narratives of power and truth that I have studied here readily resurface in the life of Jesus and in the testimony of the early church.

Moses

I have concluded my discussion of the Moses-Pharaoh interface of power and truth with reference to Mark 6:51–52:
"And they were utterly astounded, for they did not understand about the loaves, but their hearts were hardened."
These verses attest to the obtuseness of the disciples who
did not understand that the Eucharistic feeding-miracles
were exhibits of a new world that had begun; the creation
had been jump-started with abundance by the presence and
action of Jesus. The connection between the old narrative of
Pharaoh and the present wonder is the phrase "hard hearts."
The disciples could not compute the meaning of the abundance of loaves (see Mark 8:21). They were prevented from
understanding by their hard hearts. Their hard hearts replicated the hard heart of Pharaoh who, in his anxiety, had
dreamed of famine, even when he had more than enough
(Gen. 41:1–32).[4] That is, Pharaoh dreamed scarcity, a nightmare that led to his extravagant construction of store-house
cities that depended on cheap, exploited labor. The disciples
could not understand the new wave of God-given, abundant
loaves until and unless they departed their pharaonic ideology of scarcity. But the totalizing claim of scarcity excluded
for them any discernment of the new abundance enacted by
Jesus. Indeed, the narrative account of the disciples cannot
be fully understood without reference to the old pharaonic
obtuseness of hard hearts.

Solomon

In the biblical tradition Solomon represents the acme of
splendor, wealth, wisdom, power, and glory. Except it all

quickly unraveled! I have come to think that the fool in the parable of Luke 12:16–21 is none other than Solomon, who endlessly expanded his barns to store his massive wealth. Given such a provisional narrative identity, it is no wonder that Jesus, in his subsequent reflective instruction to his disciples on anxiety and trust, features Solomon as a quintessential embodiment of anxiety. Thus the birds and the flowers are offered by Jesus as anxiety-free creatures who are contrasted with the anxiety of Solomon: "Consider the lilies, how they grow: they neither toil nor spin; yet I tell you, even Solomon in all his glory was not clothed like one of these" (Luke 12:27).

Solomon, the accumulator, is portrayed in the old narrative of 1 Kings as endlessly in pursuit of more commodities (see 1 Kgs. 10:14–25). We are free to imagine, in this context, that he worried about food and clothing (Luke 12:22–23). His practice of accumulation, we are told, is a dead end because his power was remote from the truth that might have led him to a different practice of power. But his anxiety precluded such discernment.

Elisha

Elisha is a figure of legend. This means that his pastoral performance is narrated in fairy tales that live beneath the radar of royal reason and royal management and that lack credibility according to that royal reason. Elisha rarely confronts royal power in the northern kingdom of Israel but simply proceeds in his own inscrutable capacity as a transformative agent in the practical, daily, bodily life of Israel. His capacity for transformative action is said to be because he is empowered by the spirit of Elijah that is a subset of the power of God's own spirit (2 Kgs. 2:15). Everywhere this strange, inexplicable agent goes, transformative things happen: people eat (2 Kgs. 4:42–44); lepers are restored to health (2 Kgs. 5:14); wars are interrupted (2 Kgs. 6:23); and famines are ended (2 Kgs. 7:16). The narrative, of course, never tells us how. It is enough to hear the account of such specific transactions that fall completely outside the purview and the capacity of the kings who are barely visible on the horizon of the narratives (see 2 Kgs. 5:7; 6:21–22, 26–27).

In the New Testament, Elisha's transformative healing of the Syrian general from leprosy is cited as an antecedent for Jesus' own work (Luke 4:27). I have chosen, however, to suggest a connection with the narrative of Luke 7:18–22, wherein John inquires about Jesus' identity and status. John sent his inquiry about Jesus when he is imprisoned by Herod. Thus the narrative is laden with the reality of imperial power. The question from John in prison is whether there is power that gives hope for life beyond the totalizing reach of Herod and his Roman guarantors. His is an urgent practical question. The answer given by Jesus to John is one that might have been on the lips of Elisha. If he had been asked about his mandate, Elisha might have given the same response with reference to concrete practical transformations:

> "Go and tell John what you have seen and heard: the blind receive their sight, the lame walk, the lepers are cleansed, the deaf hear, the dead are raised, the poor have good news brought to them." (Luke 7:22)

The transformations wrought by Jesus (as by Elisha) are beyond dispute in that narrative world and are, at the same time, inexplicable. John can draw his own conclusions from the narrative accounts. And the Roman authorities can, and no doubt will, draw their own conclusions as well. But the theological conclusion that he is the Messiah is not the primary point of the exchange. What is primary is whether there is an effective truth that is beyond the reach of the imperial power of Rome. So it is with Elisha; his power is beyond the reach of the throne in Samaria. In both cases—Elisha and Jesus—the narrative never explains. Because explanations belong to the domain of imperial power with its regimented, administered, controlled categories of knowledge. Clearly the truth of Elisha and of Jesus is beyond such explanatory regimentation.

Josiah

The case of Josiah is very different because Josiah belongs to the Davidic line. He belongs properly to the orbit of conventional power. What startles us is that King Josiah is responsive to and positively engaged with the thrust of truth as given in the scroll. We are given no clue as to why he is amenable and responsive. There is nothing in the royal recital that prepares him for such an engagement or that prepares us as his readers. He is, in a sense, a sport of nature, a *novum* who left some in Israel dazzled by him, as he no doubt left others deeply disappointed.

It is not clear how to make a nice, direct move from Josiah to the New Testament as I have been able to do in the case of the other three narratives under consideration. To be sure, Jesus himself, as king, is attentive to the least. And if the scroll of Josiah is indeed some form of Deuteronomy as seems clear enough, then it is equally clear that Jesus, like Josiah, is a child of Deuteronomy, as is evident in his three-fold Deuteronomic response to the tempter in Luke 4:

"One does not live by bread alone."
(Luke 4:4; Deut. 8:4)

"Worship the Lord your God,
and serve only him."
(Luke 4:8; Deut. 6:4–5)

"Do not put the Lord your God to the test."
(Luke 4:12; Deut. 6:16)

Beyond that, Jesus seeks to direct his followers into a practice of faith that will defy the dominant authorities, Roman or Jewish.[5] I suggest that the familiar parable in Matthew 25:31–46 is a connection to the narrative of Josiah, a parable that connects the imagery of the end time with the least. While it may be that the parable, as John Donahue proposes, meant by the least the Christian brothers and sisters in need, there is nonetheless a connection with Josiah.[6] We are told concerning Josiah:

Did not your father eat and drink
    and do justice and righteousness?
Then it was well with him.
He judged the cause of the poor and needy;
    then it was well.
Is not this to know me?
says the LORD.
                              (Jer. 22:15–16)

This poetry concerning Josiah connects attentiveness to the least with prosperity, as does the parable. Matthew may, in the first instance, have focused on the poor and needy in the Christian community. But of course we regularly push beyond that to other poor and needy—the ones excluded from economic access, political leverage, and liturgical legitimacy. Insofar as Matthew is a Jewish Gospel, with its attentiveness to the Torah, the witness of Jesus is surely congruent with the scroll of Deuteronomy that evoked Josiah's reformative work. It is all about the least!

Thus these several narratives concerning power and truth in the Old Testament run toward the New Testament. They do not run exclusively toward the New Testament, for clearly Judaism (as a companion movement) makes the same parallel interpretive moves. In each of these narratives that I have reviewed there is something continually gnawing and surprising and haunting and compelling about the truth of God that causes and evokes these narratives of transformation in the life of the body politic. We belated readers are invited to carry, extend, and extrapolate from that ancient narrative testimony toward our own time, place, and circumstance.

CAN OLD TESTAMENT CHARACTERS SPEAK TO PRESENT-DAY POWER?

There are no easy or obvious connections to our time, place, and circumstance. But of course the question cannot be avoided. We do well, in the wake of these narratives, to reflect on power and truth in our present context of faith.

We live, I propose, in a totalizing environment. The huge concentration of power and wealth in the hands of a small number of predators—reinforced by a government that is responsive to that concentration of wealth and power and very much legitimated by establishment religion—has created an environment that contains all the socio-economic possibilities and yields an ideology of conformity that is expressed as consumerism and supported by the mantras of militarism. It becomes, in such a context, exceedingly difficult to sustain action (or even thought!) outside of that totality. For current thought or action is, for the most part, skillfully co-opted for the totality.

Robert Lifton has recently written his own life story of engagement with totalism, variously concerned with the fears of the nuclear threat, the savagery of the Vietnam War, killings in Hiroshima, and atrocities of Auschwitz.[7] He details the "atrocity-producing" systems of totalism and, from his study, has formulated the "eight deadly sins of totalism" that recur in the systems that he has studied:

> I came to view them as the "eight deadly sins" of totalism. They were: *milieu control*, that of virtually all communication in an environment; *mystical manipulation*, maneuvers from above by an obscure but ultimate authority under the guise of group spontaneity; *the demand for purity*, imposed pursuit of absolute good in order to defeat absolute evil; *the cult of confession*, obsession with continuous all-encompassing and ever-critical self-revelation; *the sacred science*, claim to doctrinal truth that is both divine and scientifically proven; *loading the language*, the reduction of all human problems to definitive-sounding phrases, to the thought-terminating cliché; *doctrine over person*, a primacy so absolute that any doubts about prevailing dogma must be considered a form of personal deficiency or psychological aberration; and *the dispensing of existence,* the sharp line drawn between those who have a right to exist and those who possess no such right. This last feature of ideological totalism for me summed up its larger evil. The "dispensing" in question could involve no more than positions offered or denied in society, or it could mean killing those considered to be tainted by the wrong background or wrong thoughts.[8]

Each of these totalities that he has studied has featured a brutalizing, controlling absolutism in which the capacity to act or think outside the totalism became exceedingly difficult.

I have no wish, *mutatis mutandis,* to draw too close an analogue to our own time or to overstate the totalizing aspects of the present American system. Except to notice that the present concentration of power and wealth among us, the collusion of much of the media, and the alliance of the courts make it possible to think that totalizing is ready at hand among us. Those of us who attend to and mean to adhere to the testimony of truth in the biblical tradition are left with the quite practical question concerning the performance of truth that concerns emancipation and transformation in a context that does not intend any emancipation from dominant ideology and that intends transformation only inside that system.

The wonderment among us is that there are agents of truth who find daring, risky ways out beyond the totalism. Sometimes (many times?) the church colludes with the totalism and blesses it, to its own considerable benefit. But sometimes the church—in feeble or in daring ways, in conventional or in imaginative ways—has an alternative say. That alternative say is regularly constituted by

- hearing the cry of the oppressed as did the God of the burning bush,
- exploring the futility of absolutism as did the ironic renderers of Solomon,
- living outside the royal surveillance in order to transform the human community as did Elisha, and
- letting old truth touch contemporary public policy in reformative ways, as did Josiah.

When that much of an alternative say is enacted, it is enough to permit one to believe in God yet again. It is finally the God of all truth who breaks the grip of totalism, who confounds the imperial governor, and who makes all things new . . . here and there . . . now and then.

LIVING AS DISCIPLES AND CITIZENS

It is important to continue to expect this old narrative to yield new renderings that pertain to us in present circumstances. New readings, however, are easy enough. We are left, in the process of engaging the text, with the vexation of being at the same time disciples *and* citizens, summoned by the Holy truth of God, but tax-paying beneficiaries of the present regime. Citizenship, however, does not require or entail subscription to the full force of the dominant ideology that now occupies center stage among us. It is clear, is it not, that our body politic has lost its way:

- lost its way in its easy violence against the vulnerable
- lost its way in its uncritical exploitation of the less entitled
- lost its way in its easy commitment to greed as a way of life
- lost its way in false promises of happiness and security
- lost its way in its presumption about entitlement and privilege as the chosen people

A society that has lost its way may indeed be ready for serious discipleship that informs citizenship. Such deep obedience to the truth that marks discipleship does not aim, in citizenship, to transpose the body politic into the church or into a theocracy. It aims rather to insist that the holy truth voices gifts and commands that matter in a society that depends too much on greed against neighbor, that practices too much denial about the crisis in the neighborhood, and that ends too much in despair.

Whenever it can, social power will tend as soon as possible toward totalism. Such social totalism is always a breath away from totalitarianism in which the exercise of genuine human freedom as a member of the community is limited, if not prohibited. When it can, totalism will offer itself as a "Final Solution" that depends on a "Final Reading" of the old tradition. But what truth and its practitioners know is that there is no Final Solution, just as there is no Final Reading of the old tradition. There are only provisional solutions that are informed by provisional readings of the old tradition. It is the work of disciples, surely, to practice that provisional: always to subvert what is failing, always to watch for new possibility that is deeply given by the holiness of God.

READING AS CONTESTANTS, LIVING AS CONTESTANTS

While I have cited other texts abut discipleship, I conclude by suggesting that the book of Acts is a vivid attestation that discipleship (now apostleship) takes place amid empire. These early Christians, infused with Easter truth, could not be stopped in their joyous public life together.

- They were *filled with the Spirit*, the force of truth that refused the citizenship of business as usual.
- They testified frequently and boldly to their Easter alternative truth *in front of imperial authorities.*
- They *told the truth* about the world in a way that subverted the world of settled power—political, economic, and religious.

They knew about establishment power in its nervous bewilderment concerning the great public questions in front of it. They denied the authority of the empire concerning ultimate questions—the kind that every totalism tries to preempt—by bearing witness to an alternative truth that centers in the resurrection of Jesus, an enactment of God's truth. They attested that God's will for life is stronger than the will for death practiced by the empire. In their testimony before the authorities they were finishing the answer to the Roman governor left unspoken in the trial of Jesus.

I am led to a fresh appreciation of the truth-telling of the witnesses in the book of Acts before the imperial authorities by the shrewd discussion of Kavin Rowe. Rowe shows the way in which the book of Acts presents these early witnesses to attest the truth of Easter as a practical truth that is evidenced by the practice of the church that confounds and contradicts the practice of the empire:

> But in saying that Acts is a narrative that can render "untrue" other narratives that offer substantially different schemes of life—that tell the human story in such a way as to say "your entire life should be lived in this way"— I am also attempting to point toward something more comprehensive or "thicker" than the sense we get from simple everyday occurrences of the word "true," namely, the truth of a habit of being, a kind of true total way of life whose pattern can be falsified by living in a fundamentally different way. We may call this the practical contour or shape of truth.[9]

Such truth

> was no doubt "open speaking" but it was also "living." . . . the term "truth claim" is to be understood as something that carries with it a way of life. At its most basic level, a

truth claim in this sense points not to an isolated statement to which one gives or withholds assent but to an entire mode of being into which one enters or does not.[10]

Rowe frames his discussion so that the attestation of the book of Acts is a refutation of polytheism and its concomitant tolerance as he construes the context of the book of Acts. For purposes of this discussion, however, I would see this testimony as a challenge to the totalism of the empire against which the apostles voice an alternative claim. The apostles find a way to testify, in talk and in walk, about a truth that is vigorously and resolutely outside the totalism of Rome. The conclusion of the book of Acts reports on Paul preaching in Rome, welcoming all and "proclaiming the kingdom of God" (5:31). Paul made a witness that excluded none. And he taught of a rule that contradicted the rule of Rome, the very locus of his own preaching. Finally, in verse 31, we are told that he bore his witness "about the Lord Jesus Christ with all boldness and without hindrance." Richard Cassidy suggests that there surely were efforts by Roman authorities to impede Paul's preaching and that the last word of the book of Acts is better translated as "unintimidated":

> Because they know unalterably that Jesus is Lord and because they also know that earthly kingdoms and empires are subject to Satan's orchestration, Luke's paradigmatic readers are well prepared to appreciate the nobility of Acts' final scene in which chained Paul continues to preach about God's kingdom and to teach that Jesus Christ is Lord—with all boldness; not intimidated![11]

Cassidy connects this final narrative report by Luke to the opening of his narrative in Luke 1:32–33 wherein Gabriel announces to Mary concerning her son to be born:

"He will be great, and will be called the Son of the Most High, and the Lord God will give to him the throne of his ancestor David. He will reign over the house of Jacob forever, and of his kingdom there will be no end." (1:32–33)

While Gabriel's announcement says not a word about Caesar's kingdom, the proclamation that Jesus' kingdom is *eternal* may implicitly raise a question about the duration of Caesar's kingdom.[12]

It occurs to me that the situation of the church in our society, perhaps the church everywhere always, is entrusted with a truth that is inimical to present power arrangements. The theological crisis in the church—that shows up in preaching and in worship as elsewhere—is that the church has largely colluded with the totalism of the National Security State. Or more broadly, has uncritically colluded with Enlightenment reason that stands behind the National Security State that makes preaching Easter an epistemological impossibility.[13] Unlike Paul, the church is in such a posture that it is not likely to be bold or unhindered; that is, it is not likely to be unintimidated. This is now clear to anyone who thinks that the totalizing claims of the National Security State have failed and been shown to be false. It is thus a time when the truth of God's victory over death invites fresh articulation and enactment—at its best, unintimidated. The several cases I have cited here—Moses, Solomon's ironic commentators, Elisha, Josiah—are consistently unintimidated. The truth that is variously enacted by such agents is not an idea or a proposition. It is rather a habit of life that simply (!) refuses the totalizing claims of power. The governor, on behalf of the empire, will continue to ask, "What is truth?" And the apostles will continue to give answer, uncommonly unintimidated: "'We must obey God rather than any human authority'" (Acts 5:29).[14]

NOTES

1. See Walter Brueggemann, *Solomon: Israel's Ironic Icon of Human Achievement* (Columbia: University of South Carolina Press, 2005).

2. That Pharaoh must give answer is evident in the formula, "That you may know that the earth is the LORD's" (Exod. 9:29). To "know" is to acknowledge sovereignty; see the negative counterpart in Exodus 5:2: "I do not know."

3. See Richard A. Horsley, *Paul and Empire: Religion and Power in Roman Imperial Society* (Harrisburg, PA: Trinity Press International, 1997).

4. On Pharaoh's hard heart, see Exodus 4:21; 8:15, 32, 34; 9:22; 10:1, 20, 27; 11:10; 14:4, 8, 17.

5. See Stanley E. Porter and Cynthia Long Westfall, *Empire in the New Testament* (Eugene, OR: Pickwick Publications, 2011).

6. John R. Donahue, *The Gospel in Parable* (Philadelphia: Fortress Press, 1988), 120–23.

7. Robert Jay Lifton, *Witness to an Extreme Century: A Memoir* (New York: Free Press, 2011).

8. Ibid., 67–68; see also p. 381.

9. C. Kavin Rowe, *World Upside Down: Reading Acts in the Graeco-Roman Age* (Oxford: Oxford University Press, 2009), 161.

10. Ibid., 161–62.

11. Richard J. Cassidy, "Paul's Proclamation of *Lord* Jesus as a Chained Prisoner in Rome," *Luke-Acts and Empire: Essays in Honor of Robert L. Brawley,* ed. David Rhoads et. al. (Eugene, OR: Pickwick Publications, 2011), 153.

12. Ibid., 151.

13. Chalmers Johnson, *The Sorrows of Empire: Militarism, Secrecy, and the End of the Republic* (New York: Henry Holt, 2005), enumerates the high costs of the National Security State, which includes perpetual war, bottomless debt, and loss of civil rights.

14. John Calvin, *Institutes of the Christian Religion* 4.20.32; ed. John T. McNeill, trans. Ford Lewis Battles, LCC (Philadelphia: Westminster Press, 1960), 2:1521, cites this text as a final citation. Of the text he writes:

> let us comfort ourselves with the thought that we are rendering that obedience which the Lord requires when we

suffer anything rather than turn aside from piety. And that our courage may not grow faint, Paul pricks us with another goad: That we have been redeemed by Christ at so great a price as our redemption cost him, so that we should not enslave ourselves to the wicked desires of men—much less be subject to their impiety [I Cor. 7:23].